Methods of Evaluation in Physical Education

By
Dr. PALA JOHNSON
M.P.Ed., Ph.D.
Physical Director,
Government Junior College,
Old Town
Anantapur (AP)—515 005

Discovery Publishing House
New Delhi

First Published-2001
Reprinted-2011
ISBN 81-7141-620-9

Published by :
DISCOVERY PUBLISHING HOUSE
4831/24, Ansari Road, Prahlad Street,
Daryaganj, New Delhi-110002 (INDIA)
☎ : 3279245 • Fax : 91-11-3253475
E-mail : dphtemp@indiatimes.com

Printed at:
Mehra Offset Press
Delhi

CONTENTS

PREFACE

The approach to measurement in Physical Education should be the terms of improved services to boys and girls. If the terms is acceptable, the selection and use of test should be ultimately related to the purposes designed to realise those purpose. Thus, tests would be utilised to and in the educational process. In certain respects, each persons is unique, differing in many ways from others in background and capabilities. Physical education should understood each person needs in order to give adequate guidance and to adapt programmes to keep those needs. Successful measurement then involves defining and evaluating the truly important outcomes of physical education—that is, the abilities, needs, and capacities of individual pupils. The appropriate use of test results should make teaching and training more effective.

Measurement is a universal practice since it is employed in all fields of endeavour and used in its varied forms by all individuals. Test and measurement are part of the technology produced by the research in the discipline. Scientifically constructed test have been developed through research in fitness, motor ability, sports skills, knowledge and values, and these have become valuable as components of the teaching and learning process.

One of the chief functions of education is to understand the student and an important purpose of measure is to identify and recognise needs that will help in that understanding. Student differs in many ways. However, these differences can be translated to identify the gifted student.

In sports and physical education, as in life, teacher and coaches are constantly measuring and evaluating . They measure their students, players, associates, opponents, programme, teaching strategies, coaching teachniques, and many other facts of the educational continuum. The most valid form is the use of well established criteria as a basis for comparison. Usually this is done by means of tests and measures, that have been developed through research and validated against suitable criteria.

By accepting the above facts the author concentrated more about the need of physical education in relation to test, measurement and evaluating. He felt that the role of physical education teacher is vital in identifying the talents of the pupil. He should be trained well and should possess the knowledge regarding physical fitness. construction of tests to identify the various physical abilities and process of evaluation.

In this book, the author very clearly discussed the way of construction of tests to identify the physical fitness abilities and statistical analysis to construct the norms (standards) for the tests to compare the abilities. It helps the physical education teachers and coaches to identify the students' efficiency which will be the base for admission to various programmes of physical education and sports.

ACKNOWLEDGEMENTS

The present study has been undertaken with the generous help and guidance of several of my teachers, friends colleagues and my family members at different stages. I express my sincere gratitude and thanks to all of them.

I am extremely happy to express my heartfelt gratitude to my teacher and research guide Prof. P. Chinnappa Reddy, who has been instrumental in developing zeal for the subject in me. He has prompted me to take up research work in the field of Physical Education. Without his encouragement and guidance this piece of work would have been impossible. I am extremely grateful to him for his constant efforts for my development.

I am extremely thankful to Sri C. Lokanath Reddy, Associate Professor and Head of Computer Science, S.K. University for his valuable suggestions and guidance S.K. University and my friend selecting to computer application for the study work.

I specially thank Dr. K. Satyanarayana Reddy, Assistant Professor of Economics, S.K. University, Prof. K.L.A.P. Sharma, Professor of Statistics, S.K. University, Dr. P. Satyanarayana Reddy, Lecturer in Physical Education, Govt. Junior College, Sri Kalahasthi, and Dr. P. Raghunandan, Lecturer in Physical Education, Govt. Junior College, Khammam, for giving their valuable suggestions and guidance during the execution of this research work.

My sincere thanks are also due to Prof. B.R. Vijaya Rao, Professor of Physical Education, Nagarjuna University, Guntur, Prof. D.P. Jaya Kumar, Professor of Physical Education, S.V. University, Tirupati, Prof. Vaidyanathan, Professor and Head, Department of Physical Education, Annamalai University and Dr. Ravindran, Associate Professor of Physical Education, Annamalai University, Chidambaram for helping me in data collection and for giving me advice.

My affectionate regards are due to Dr. P. Murali Krishna, Associate Professor of Management, S.K.University, Dr. P. Ravi Kumar, Assistant Professor of Physical Education, R.E.C, Warangal, Mr. N. Ravindranath, Assistant Registrar, S.K. University College, Mr. J.J.Soloman, Mr. Titus Paul, Mr. Paul, Anantapur and host of my friends for their continuous support for my academic endeavours.

I thank the Department of Physical Education and the authorities of S.K. University for allowing to make use of infrastructure and other facilities required for the study.

My special thanks to Mr. Raghunatha Reddy and my sister P. Mary Emelia for their excellent skills shown in typing the thesis.

I thank my wife Smt. V. Hymavathi for showing monumental patience and for extending invaluable support throughout the preparation of the thesis.

I thank all those who have generously helped me directly or indirectly in making this study possible.

Finally, I alone assume that responsibility for any errors and omissions that might have been committed unconsciously.

(P. JOHNSON)

CHAPTER—1

INTRODUCTION

"Physical Education may be defined as an education through the physical activities where many of the educational objectives are achieved by means of big muscle play activities. It is a vital phase of education and an integral part of the total educational process"[1].

The vital phase of education, that is physical education, aims at all round development of an individual where the medium of achieving the goal is physical activity. Hence it is through the big muscle-play activity an individual can enlighten the personality traits such as physical fitness, emotional balance and social behaviour etc., besides intellectual development.

The physical education programme provides each student with an opportunity to assess his fitness, and to develop skill and understanding that will enable him to enjoy a productive stay in school/college and a more meaningful existence after school/college.

In a broad view of education, physical education has unique opportunities for developing desirable character and social traits as well as defined responsibilities toward the physical development of the individual. A person physically fit will be mentally alert and sound and will be more spectacular in all walks of his life. A weak child is a weak brick in the wall of the nation. If today's child is weak and meek, he is considered as a liability not only to his family and himself but also to the entire nation. The wealth of a nation depends entirely upon the health of every citizen of the country.

In the American College of Sports Medicine, Steinhaus,[2] former Dean of George Williams College stated that, Even as every pagoda needs a strong foundation to carry its beautiful superstructure, so every person must be possessed of physical fitness to support the burdens that life will force on him. But as we look upward we find that every pagoda culminates in a point that is directed to heavens. It is as though the entire structure is for the purpose of permitting this upward thrust that transforms a mere wooden structure into pagoda. So also man's entire being must support an upward thrust which is giving purpose to his life, transforms man the animal, into man and human being, 'Know thyself'[3] is a phrase that is familiar to all. It is an ancient precept quoted by an American poet and philosopher in his essay 'The American Scholar' From a practical standpoint, it is essential that every one should evaluate realistically his/her talents and limitations. It is important for their welfare that they neither grossly underestimate nor overestimate their capacities and capabilities.

In order to do this one should need some means of getting information about himself. Psychology provides intelligence and aptitude tests for guidance. A simple mirror or perhaps some candid photographs frequently tell how one looks to others. A visit to the physicians helps to get good idea of his/her status with respect to disease and physical degeneration.

There is, however, the need for a little more information about oneself to do an adequate job of problem solving and decision making in terms of personal health and fitness.

For this reason, one should participate in a series of tests which will provide a realistic profile of his/her. Every one should take an advantage of it to correct physical inadequacies and to maintain present assets effectively.

Measuring physical efficiency is just as complex a quality as intelligence to measure. Like intelligence it depends upon not a single quality, not single test. To measure physical efficiency, firstly, the parameter, which contributes to it, should be determined; secondly, an appropriate test should be selected to measure the specific parameter.

Right from the origin of Physical Education the major objectives of physical education was physical fitness. The aim of physical education in the early years attained physical fitness, which was a main requisite of the then citizens. As days changed the need, importance, scope and objectives have also changed because the demand of environment to preserve, to withstand stress, to resist fatigue and to possess the energy for vigorous and well-rounded life has increased.

Clarke[4] has rightly defined physical fitness as "The ability to carry out daily tasks with vigour and alertness, without undue fatigue, and with ample energy to engage in leisure pursuits and to meet emergency situations".

The daily tasks of different individuals differ in nature from others as their life styles, work environments and leisure pursuits are different. All individuals, have some degree of physical fitness, which varies considerably in different people and in the same person from time to time. Thus, the need of physical fitness has become a way of life in the modern society.

Here the role of a physical education teacher is vital, as he has to attend to various individuals with varying levels of physical fitness and varying levels of energy demands for carrying out their tasks. The physical educator should be competent enough to perform these highly specified tasks of attending different individuals with different traits and goals. They should be trained well and should possess the knowledge regarding physical education and its allied subjects besides being himself fit. For this purpose, the institutions, which train physical education teachers, should select the right person for the right job. As the responsibility of transferring the knowledge of physical education teachers, the institutions which train these personnel should not compromise in the principles of selecting and training these people.

When the process of selection is involved the necessity of test, measurement and evaluation arises.

"Test is a specific tool, procedure or technique used to elicit a response from the student in order to gain information to be used as a basic appraisal of the quantity or quality of elements such as fitness, skill, knowledge and values".[5]

"Measurement is a technique of evaluation that uses tests and other procedures and instruments, is generally precise and objective, normally results in quantitative data and characteristically can express its results in numerical form when indicating ability or capacity is some trait or characteristics involving fitness motor skill knowledge, value or process."[6]

"Evaluation is a process of education that uses data gathered from the product and the process by means of measurement techniques. It is expressed in either a subjective or objective manner and can be used for comparisons with preconceived criteria to make judgement."[7]

These definitions make clear that test, measurement and evaluation are not synonymous terms but are closely related to each other. Evaluation is part of the dynamic process of education, measurement is a technique of evaluation and tests are specific tools of measurement.

MEASUREMENT AND EVALUATION

Measurement and Evaluation are interdependent concepts. Evaluation is a process that uses measurement and the purpose of measurement is to collect information. Tests are made for this purpose. In the evaluation process, information is interpreted according to established standards so that clear decisions can be made. Clearly the success of evaluation depends on the quality of the data collected. If test results are not consistent and truthful, accurate evaluation is impossible. The measurement process is the first step in evaluation improved measurement leads to accurate evaluation.

The measurement of man date back to ancient civilizations and is the oldest form of measurement. It was of interest in ancient India and later in Egypt [8] where the study was undertaken to find one part or component of the body that would predict or become a common measurement of all other parts of the body.

History reveals that as man becomes more civilized, he becomes more scientific to seek more exact ways to measure. The history of measurement in physical education parallels the growth and development in research and the rise of physical education to more respected position in the educational spectrum.

Modern techniques in measurement were developed only a little over 100 years back in few countries like America.[9] Their history can be divided roughly into periods of running from about 1960 to present.

Various measurement techniques for different elements were developed in different years.

Anthroprometric measurements	-	1860-1890
Strength tests	-	1880-1910
Cardio Vascular tests	-	1990-1925
Athletic ability tests	-	1900-1930
Sports skill tests	-	1920
Knowledge tests	-	1940
Fitness tests	-	1940

Physical fitness tests were developed at the time of World War II. These tests were geared to the need of the war period. They could be mass administered, easily scored and interpreted. All branches of armed forces devised fitness tests with appropriate norms. A number of such other tests were developed for schools and college groups as well as other institutions like fire fighters, police personnel etc.

Every institution has its own purpose in conducting a test and every test has its own purpose in measuring a specific quality in individuals. The various elements of physical fitness such as strength, speed, flexibility, endurance etc., have to be measured by using various test procedures.

The selection of appropriate test is necessary when application of results is to be realized. The little time allotted for measurement activities should be made in the light of objectives sought. If the tester is a teacher, detailed, technical measurement may be desired. The teacher is just concerned about the accuracy and honesty of the results but he has to find a test that is easy to use which is appropriate to the group situation that is present in most schools. The theme is centered on helping the teacher get the effective answer with the best tools; judgement about test selection will continue to be needed as how tests become available.

According to Wayman,[10] the real physical efficiency tests must determine, and take cognizance of an individual's physical deficiencies, there must be physical or mental reasons for them, and a real physical efficiency test would tend to show the physical reason. Then using this as an intelligent basis for procedure, one can treat the primary cause before attempting to improve the motor deficiencies.

Measurement and evaluation are an integral component in acquiring knowledge about one's self, and students in a school setting clients in a non-school setting, subjects in a research setting and the general public provides information about curricula, programmes and instruction. Measurement tools and evaluation procedures can be motivating, informative and diagnostic. Frequently, the results of measurement and evaluation are used in assessing the accountability of the professional physical educator.

For years, it was assumed that students who attended the class were learning and that quality of life was enhanced. All of these assumptions may be true, but they cannot be certain unless systematic procedures are used for measurement and evaluation. Such assumptions may be very tenuous, and are likely to be challenged by parents, school officials and leaders who are concerned with making schools accountable for the learning and the development of children.

For many years, there has been interest in methods of rating and in various rating schemes. In 1861, Dr.Hitchcock of Amherst began to work in the field of Anthropometry for rating purposes. Annually, between 1861 and 1901, according to Bovard and Cozens, he published anthropometric tables of Amherst men, until finally given his age and height he had tables to show what the average college student should expect to measure, weigh, blow, push, lift etc. He was able to furnish each student after his first physical examination with a chart by which he may know at a glance whether he is near or below his estimated average so far as measurements, tests and examinations will show.[11]

Evaluation is inevitable in teaching. Like it or not, there are numerous instructional decisions that must be made and action taken accordingly. The more accurately he/she evaluates or judges his/her students and programmes, the more effective he/she will be in providing a sound educational experience.

In a general sense, the main purpose of teaching is to help students achieve desired learning outcomes in the cognitive, effective and psychomotor domains. Clearly defining the desired learning outcomes in terms of specific instructional objectives is the first step in good teaching: it is also essential in the effective evaluation of student achievement and learning.

According to Grounlund,[12] evaluation is a systematic process of determining the extent to which instructional objectives are achieved by pupils.

Though measurement is obvious to promote and improve learning, the task would not be fulfilled without proper evaluation. Testing just for the sake of testing is not only a waste of time, but also an actual obstruction in the total educational process. When measurements are conducted, there should be a guiding purpose for which the resulting data may be used. Judicious use of evaluation procedures can give the direction to teaching that cannot be obtained in any way.

Evaluation is the process of giving meaning to measurement by judging it against some standard. Two commonly used standards are: 1) criterion-referenced standard and 2) norm-referenced standard.

Criterion-referenced standard is concerned with the degree to which a student has a level of competence, it requires that the task should be defined in explicit terms.

Norm-referenced standard is based on statistical procedure, which is used to judge an individual's performance in relation to others of same age, sex and particular ability level. Therefore, norms are necessary in order to interpret the test scores, which are meaningless without this essential factor.

Many standardized tests were developed which were based on various scores and norms suitable for a specific population, age, sex or country as a show but as Ebel [13] defined "people are different that vary in body, size, shape, speed, strength and in many other respects. Measurements determine the degree to which an individual possesses a defined characteristic. It involves first characteristic to be measured and then selecting the instrument with which to measure it".

So the test which is intended to measure a particular group should be designed suitably for that group and the norms and standards should be fixed accordingly. Many test batteries like AAHPER youth fitness test. AAHPER Sports Skill Test, Indiana motor fitness test, Texas Physical fitness motor ability test, National Physical efficiency test etc., have become universally acceptable and are being applied as devices of measurements in various institutions, states all over the world. Do these tests really test their efficiency? In the sense does a test constructed which is based on the scores of a particular population, be administered somewhere else in the world on different population? Do the local conditions influence or effect these studies? Such questions arise when we go deep into the testing procedures practised in various institutes in India.

Physical education colleges all over India apply different testing procedures for selecting candidates for admission into there institutes for different educational courses they offer. Are those tests standard? For example, the YMCA College of Physical Education, Channai conducts a physical efficiency test for students aspiring for its Bachelor of Physical Education Degree Course, which includes items such as 100mts. run 800 Mts. run, Shot Put and Broad jump. Similarly the Annamalai University in Tamilnadu has test items like 100 m. run, sit ups, pull ups, vertical jump, and 12 min. run/walk for Bachelor of Physical Education and Sports Sciences course and the same test is being administered into Master of Physical Education and Sports Sciences Course also.

Under the auspicious of state council of higher education, Government of Andhra Pradesh, Sri Krishnadevaraya University was the first University to conduct the Physical Education Common Entrance Test during 1992 and 1993 as Prof. M.J. Kesava Murthy Vice Chancellor as its Chairman and Dr. P. Chinnappa Reddy Professor and Director of Physical Education as its Convenor. The investigator of this study who is working in the Dept. of Physical Education of the above University associated in conducting Entrance test for students who are opting for various courses in Physical Education at various Colleges, has developed a sort of interest in analysing the existing test procedures and to suggest standardised norms for selecting the candidates for admission intovarious Physical Education Courses in Andhra Pradesh.

Government of Andhra Pradesh evolved a common entrance test to select students into various physical education courses of their state like Under Graduate Diploma in Physical Education (U.G.D.P.Ed). Bachelor of Physical Education (B.P.Ed) and Master of Physical Education (M.P.Ed) under the G.O.Ms.No.161, Education, 4th May, 1989. To get admission into the U.G.D.P.Ed. and B.P.Ed., courses a student should pass the physical efficiency test - According to the Andhra Pradesh Government Gazette.[14]

The following test items were framed to find out the physical efficiency of students. They are:

Men	*Women*
1) 100 Mts. Run	1) 100 Mts. Run
2) 800 Mts. Run	2) 400 Mts. Run
3) High Jump	3) High Jump
4) Long Jump	4) Long Jump
5) Shot put.	5) Shot put.

The above tests are aimed at determining the individual's speed, endurance, explosive strength etc. The aim of administering these tests is also that an individual who can perform well in these tests should possess the elements of physical fitness like speed, strength, endurance, explosive strength and these components are very much essential for a student who has to undergo a vigorous training programme in the physical education courses.

Having associated with the common entrance test called, Physical Education Common Entrance Test (P.E.C.E.T) as an tester and evaluator for five years i.e., 1992, 1993, 1994, 1995 and 1997 the investigator of this study felt that the present existing test items should be standardized and to construct norms according to the needs of the present local population and performance levels. Another important aspect where the researcher has decided to investigate is that the two particular items namely High Jump and Long Jump which require explosive strength in legs are similar in nature. So one of them may be eliminated from the test which also saves the time and feasible in administration. Either of the test items can be eliminated from the battery by finding the weightage of the items in the battery by using Statistical Procedure, 'Multiple Linear Regression Analysis' and 'Correlation Matrix'. Furthermore Investigator wants to construct the Norms for the test items both for men and women.

Keeping the above factors in mind, the researcher felt the need of the present study for investigation.

STATEMENT OF THE PROBLEM

The purpose of this study is Construction of Norms and standardizing the existing physical efficiency test items of Physical Education Common Entrance Test of Andhra Pradesh.

DELIMITATIONS

The study was delimited to the following aspects:

1. Study was conducted on those students who appeared for the Physical Education Common Entrance Test (P.E.C.E.T) in Andhra Pradesh.
2. Both men and women students seeking admission into Bachelor of Physical Education were selected as subjects. Their age ranged from 20 to 23 years.
3. Functional relationship was established by following multiple regression analysis in the first case the functional relationship was established between criterion variable and all the other independent variable. In the second analysis high-jump was dropped and in the third long jump was eliminated because as earlier mentioned the researcher made an attempt to eliminate one of the above two variables which asses the same quality.

LIMITATIONS

The following were the limitations of the study

1. As the test was conducted at three different places of three respective regions, consists 23 districts of Andhra Pradesh., the ground conditions, climate and some other external factors might have had an effect on the study.

2. As the personnel involved in conducting the test and measuring the scores were large in number and different people were testers at different places, there may be variations in testing procedures. The tester reliability could not be established by using any standard criteria. However all the persons involved in testing and measuring procedures were well qualified people working as teachers in physical education, physical directors and coaches.
3. The tests were conducted at various places of diverse climatic and terrestrial conditions and hence the influence, if any, of the natural setup of the places of the test was not accounted for during the computation of the Norms.

DEFINITION AND EXPLANATION OF TERMS

Physical Efficiency Tests

Those objective tests used to measure learnings which include ability, motor fitness, sport skill, posture and nutrition.[15]

Physical Fitness

Fitness is that state which characterizes the degree to which a person is able to function efficiently. Fitness is an individual matter. It implies the ability of each person to live most efficiently within his potentialities.[16]

Physical Efficiency

The total functional capacity to perform some specified task requiring muscular effort: Considers the individual involved, task to be performed, quality and intensity of effort, one aspect of total fitness, involves sound organic development, motor skill and the capacity to perform physical work with biological efficiency.[17]

Test

A set of questions, problems, or exercises for determining a person's knowledge, abilities, aptitude or qualifications. A specific tool of measurement for the collection of data, implying a response from person being measured.[18]

Norms

"Norms are derived scores that are determined from the raw score obtained by a specific test".[19]

A norm is a scale that permits conversion from a raw score to a score capable of comparisons and interpretations. Norms are representations of some large population. They should be based on particular type of group that is well identified. Norms should be based on large number of cases. Other factors must be geographic location, race and skill level.[20]

PHYSICAL EDUCATION COMMON ENTRANCE TESTS (P.E.C.E.T.)

The examination conducted for assigning merit ranking to students which will be the basis for admission of the students into courses, namely Undergraduate Diploma in Physical Education (U.G.D.P.Ed.) Bachelor of Physical Education (B.P.Ed) and Master of Physical Education (M.P.Ed.) offered in various institutions of physical education, functioning under Government, Campus/ Constituent of Universities and Private Managements. This test will be conducted by the Convenor, appointed by the State Council, on different dates at different centres of three regions of Andhra Pradesh as specified by the State Council in consultation with the Chairman of Entrance Test Committee.[21]

For this study the data of men and women students seeking admission into B.P.Ed. course was considered. The items of the physical efficiency test were 100 mts., 800 mts. (400 mts. for women), High-jump, Long-jump and shot-put.

SIGNIFICANCE OF THE STUDY

1. The result of this study may help in construction of norms and standardize the test items for future Common Entrance Test.
2. The study will help in the selection of suitable students to get admission into the physical education profession it provides standards on physical education programme.

3. Based on the results, the number of test items may be altered as per the requirement.
4. This study may contribute to the knowledge of physical education in general and test measurement and evaluation in particular.
5. The results and finding of the study can be submitted to the Government and necessary action can be recommended.

Finally, it will help the physical education personnel to diagnosis the strength and weakness of pupils, to measure their fitness growth and use the test results for other instructional and guidance purposes.

REFERENCES

1. Harold M. Barrow, Rose Mary Mc Gee. "A Practical Approach to Measurement in Physical Education", 3rd Ed. (Philadelphia: Lea & Febigal, 1979), p.6.
2. Arthur H. Steinhaus, "The Challenge of Health Education to the YMCA" cited by Wynn F. Updyke and Perry B. Johnson, Principles of Modern Physical Education, Health and Recreation (New York: Holt, Rinehart and Winston Inc., 1970) p.29.
3. Emerson R.W. "The American Schools, ed. American Literature of the Nineteenth Century" An Anthology: Eurasia Publishing House (Pvt.) Ltd., New Delhi (1955) p.48.
4. H. Harrison Clarke, "Definition of Physical Fitness" Journal of Physical Education and Recreation, 50, No.8 (Oct. 1979) p.28.
5. Harold M. Barrow., Rose Mary Mc Gee., "A Practical Approach to Measurement in Physical Education", 3rd Ed. (Philadelphia: Leas & Febiger, 1979), p.7.
6. Ibid.
7. Ibid.
8. Cureton T.K., "Physical Fitness Appraisal and Guidance", (St. Lous: The C.V. Mosby Co., 1947), p.397.
9. W.L. Foster, : "A Test of Physical Efficiency", American Physical Education Review, 19:132 (1941).

10. Agnes R. Wayman, "Testing and Scoring the Physical Efficiency of College Women", Research Quarterly, 1 (1930), p.75.

11. Agnes R. Wayman "What to Measure in Physical Education", Research Quarterly, 1 (1930), p.97.

12. N.E. Gronlund, Measurement and Evaluation in Teaching (4th ed.) cited by Larry O.Hensley, "Current Measurement and Evaluation Practices in Professional PE", Journal of Physical Education, Recreation and Dance, 61, 3 (1990), p.32.

13. Ebel., "Measuring Educational Achievement" as mentioned by Clarke & Clarke in Application of Measurement to Physical Education (New Jersey: Prentice Hall, 1987), p.13.

14. The Andhra Pradesh Gazette (Published by authority, No.22, May 1989). Government of Andhra Pradesh.

15. Ted A. Baugartner, Andrew S. Jackson., "Measurement for Evaluation in Physical Education and Exercise Science", 3rd Ed. (lowa: W.C. Brown Pub., 1982), p.276.

16. Hockey, Physical Fitness: A Pathway to Healthful Living, p.8.

17. M.D. Hunter, "A Dictionary for Physical Education", (Bhoomington: Indian University Press, 1966).

18. Barrow Harold M., Mc Gee Rose Mary, "A Practical approach to measurement in Physical Education", 3rd Ed. (Philadelphia: Lea & Febiger, 1979), p.578.

19. Margaret J. Safrit, "Evaluation in Physical Education Assessing Motor Behaviour", (Englewood Cliffs, New Jersey: Prentice Hall Inc., 1981), p.243.

20. Harold M. Barrow and Rose Mary Mc Gee, "A Practical Approach to Measurement in Physical Education", (2nd Ed.) (Philadelphia: Lea & Febiger, 1979), p.45.

21. The Andhra Pradesh Gazette, (Published by the Authority No.22, Hyderabad, 1989).

CHAPTER—2

REVIEW OF RELATED LITERATURE

As a Researcher, in his personal discussion and association with the Convenor of the Physical Education Common Entrance Test, he felt the need to construct norms and to standardise the Physical Efficiency test items for admission to various courses of Physical Education offered by the Colleges of Physical Education in Andhra Pradesh. The Researcher has personally verified and studied.

A review of related literature available in the libraries of the Department of Physical Education, Sri Krishnadevaraya University, Anantapur, Department of Physical Education, Annamalai University, Chidambaram, and the Department of Physical Education, Alagappa University, Karaikudi, which are considered to be relevant is presented in this chapter.

Under the Chairmanship of Paul A.Hunsicker,[1] a Committee of the Research Council of the American Alliance for Health, Physical Education, Recreation and Dance, as it now known, selected seven test items, each representing a set of different motor fitness components to compare the AAHPERD Youth Fitness Test. The Battery consists of seven items, they are push-up for boys, flexible arm hang for girls, straight knee sit-ups, shuttle run, standing long jump, soft ball throw for distance, 50 yard dish, 600-yard run/walk. Revision of the youth fitness test were made in 1965 and again in 1975, with some changes in 1976; the final test manual was proposed by Hunsicker and Reiff. The following changes were ultimately made in the original battery. Softball distance throw was eliminated, Bent-knee sit-up in one minute replaced ultimate sit-up.

Glover,[2] developed test items for the first, second and third grades. After examining performance items that could be utilised in a motor fitness test battery, eighteen tests were chosen. These tests were evaluated on two occasions by individuals familiar with physical fitness and with primary school children. On the first occasion, the judges indicated either selection, need for revision, or rejection of each test, as a result, twelve items were retained for further consideration. On the second occasion, the judges made evaluation while the tests were being administered to children. As a consequence seven tests composed the final selection. Percentile norms were developed for all seven items for all grades continued. However, the fourth test was found to be most valid, reliable, and discriminatory. The test items are Standing Broad Jump, sit-up, and shuttle race and seal curl.

At Purdue University, Arnett,[3] developed short motor fitness test batteries for high school girls. The Battery found test was composed of three items modified pull-ups, 600-yard run, and standing broad jump. This battery had a validity coefficient 0.755 and an estimated reliability coefficient of 0.848. In addition Ismail and his associate have studied motor fitness test for college men based upon factor analysis of a comprehensive coverage of components and test items.

Holding and Jackson,[4] conducted a study on physical fitness. The norm-reflected standards were developed from scores of over 1500 men and women, who were tested at different Young Men's Christian Association throughout the United States. The standards included the test scores associated with selected percentiles. A percential was the percentage of people of a given age group and gender who achieved the score. A maximal oxygen uptake of 54ml/kg. minimum fell in the ninety fifth percentile for men in the age group of thirty five years and below. This means that of all men tested who have 35 years and younger ninety five per cent had an average score of 54 ml/kg. minimum or lower and only five per cent had an average score of more than 54 ml/kg. minimum.

Brouha and Ball,[5] made a further modification of the Harvard step test for use with elementary school boys and girls. The bench was lowered in height to 14 inches. The stepping times were changed by ages; two minutes for seven years, three minutes for eight to twelve years. Scoring and classification and the same as for college men in the original test of Harvard step test.

Mood,[6] conducted a study of two forms of the test of physical fitness, knowledge of senior physical education for major students. One hundred and eighty four experimental test items, the contents of which were based on 60 physical fitness facts secured from recent physical education literature and on the opinions of 73 members of the Research Council of AAHPER, were administered to 1,360 physical education major students enrolled in 35 collegiate institutions in the United States. As a result of item analysis data, two parallel forms of the tests were constructed. For the purpose of obtaining validity and reliability of data and establishing national norms the two final test forms were administered to 4,167 students enrolled in 150 collegiate institutions in the United States. Two forms of the test of physical fitness knowledge were constructed so that growth in comparison of physical fitness can be analyzed.

The recent development of health related fitness test constituted a shift in the concept of fitness testing. The most prominent of these in the AAPHERD test, a manual,[7] was published in 1980 and a manual,[8] was published in 1984 prior proposals for the script of test were evident in Texas. South Carolina, and elsewhere, will be mentioned later in this chapter. A committee was appointed in 1975 to review and possibility to revise the AAHPHERD Youth Fitness Test; represented on this committee were the physical fitness, research and measurement and evaluation council of the Association for Research, Administration, Professional Council and Societies, AAHPHERD. Instead of revising youth fitness test, the committee recommended that a health-related physical fitness test should be constructed. The AAHPHERD Health related physical fitness test contains four items intended to assess as individuals status on three components of health related physical fitness tests. Items are mile run or distance run in 9 minutes, triceps skin fold, modified situps and sit and reach.

Falls,[9] established norms on the AAHPHERD youth physical fitness. The norms were computed for more than 10,000 young subjects. Those who fall below the 50th percentile in any area were advised to participate in a fitness-developed programme.

In 1973, the Texas[10] Governor's Commission on physical fitness published the Texas Physical fitness and motor ability battery in 1985 and 1986. The health-related portion of the test was under revision. The revision was through the combination effort of public school physical educators and leading medical, fitness, and health and measurement specialists. National fitness and medical experts reviewed the test. In 1985 and 1986 the test was scheduled for extensive pilot research. Test items are, steady start run, curl-up, sit and reach, body composition.

Fletcher,[11] conducted a study of physical fitness using AAHPERD youth fitness test. In his study, 1,400 senior high school boys were selected as subjects from fifty nine schools throughout Arkanasa. It was found that six of the twelve factors investigated had significant relationship to the fitness level of the subjects. Percentile ratio for senior high school boys in Arkanasa on each item of the AAHPERD youth fitness test was also developed.

According to Agnes Wayman,[12] as early as 1894 attention was turned to the motor side of the problem. At that time the normal school Gymnastics at Milwonkee was attempting to measure student ability in nine events. In 1904 Meylan, Columbia, began to develop comprehensive test utilising the elements of running, jumping, vaulting, climbing etc. Beginning with 1908, we read of physical ability tests, efficiency test, tests for all round efficiency, average records for boys and girls as a result of certain playground efficiency test, physical education efficiency test. In 1924 Mc Curby as Chairman of a Committee on motor ability test brought out a series of tests designed to measure skill on the elements of such games as foot ball, soccer, field hockey, basket ball and tennis.Rogers in his physical capacity tests and offers proof that such tests are also a measure of athletic ability. Brace's latest work on measuring motor ability tests designed to test pure motor abilities. Finally the author suggested the following measures in physical education.

a) Native motor ability
b) Achievement in physical skills for the purpose of determining;
c) Information acquired as to technique in various fields within physical education;
d) General information in the entire field;
e) Anthropometric measurement for the purpose of determining various growth conditions;
f) Strength - General bodily strength and strength of partial muscle group;
g) General athletic ability;
h) Cordio vascular efficiency or physical fitness
i) Physical activity, habit and attitudes;
j) Posture and body mechanics.

Robson and others,[13] conducted a study on a simple fitness test battery for elementary school children, 152 boys and 150 girls of Kendriya Vidyalaya, Gwalior, studying from grade one through five acted as the subjects at random. All the subjects and assistants were oriented to the test battery comprising (1) 50 meters dash, (2) 600 meters run/walk, (3) Straight leg sit ups, (4) Vertical jump, (5) 4 x 10 meters shuttle run and (6) modified push ups. The subjects were given practice in these items so that they were able to give the correct performance in each item. The assistants were properly oriented to record measurements accurately so that mistakes could be avoided. The test items were administered to the subjects on two days, administering three items each day. After a day's rest, the test items were administered again to the same students on fourth and fifth day for finding out the reliability. The value of 'r' obtained was 0.87, which shows that the subjects had achieved consistency of performance in the test items. Norms were computed for the six physical fitness test items. The norms can be used for classifying the children into ability groups by assessing their physical fitness.

Dunder,[14] in his study was to determine the relationship of strength and motor ability and to formulate a multiple strength index for general motor ability. Solution of this problem required two sets of tests. The strength group was similar to that used by Rogers with the exception that lung capacity was omitted and the pull-up and push-up events were scored by Mecloy's method. These tests involved primary such as fundamental running, jumping, leaping, climbing, throwing etc. The motor ability tests were all scored as a comparable basis and the total composite score was used in determining, by means of multiple regressions, the relative contribution of each strength test and to find, if possible, various combination of the strength group correlating high with the composite motor ability scores. For analysis of data each of the various strength tests was correlated against total motor point. Multiple regression was worked out for various combinations of the strength test against total motor point.

Monotype and Lamphiear,[15] conducted a study on grip and arm strength in males and females. More than 6,000 males and females aged 10 to 69 in a total community in Tecumseh and Michigan, were given grip and arm strength tests. Eighty two per cent of the entire community who were in that age range participated in the study. Of this 82 percent, almost all persons without medical contradictions took the strength tests. Percentile scores for both sexes within narrow age ranges were presented. In most populations in which strength had been measured over a wide range, the participants were volunteers; hence it was not possible to define the population. Because of the high participation rate, the Tecumseh sample includes those who ordinarily would volunteer for strength tests, but also those who generally would not. Therefore the percentile scores presented probably represent arm grip strength in healthy males and females than other data which has been published.

Wendler,[16] in his study was to analyze statistically for their common and group component, forty test elements devised for use in physical education classes for boys at the high school level. Thurstone's method for determining multiple factors was utilized for this "Critical analysis of test element used in physical education". To formulate combinations of items which would give high multiple correlation with the common component. If thurstone's statement, the factor loading represent zero-order correlations with the common compounds, continues to be substantiated by further research, then the regression weightages giving high multiple correlation with these criteria will be of value as instrument for diagnostic testing and for further research he analyzed the study by using multiple factor analysis, partial and multiple correlation. Evidence presented in his report indicates the presence of four underlying common factors in test performance in the field of physical education. These factors have been identified as strength, speed of movement, motor educability and sensory motor co-ordination.

Fleishman,[17] conducted a study on thirteen tests measuring eight physical fitness factors, which were administered to over 20,000 students between the ages of 12-18 in 45 cities, distributed throughout the United States. The results of this provided (a) normative table by which individual programme can be evaluated by test, age, sex and (b) 'growth curves' which show the development of the different physical proficiency components during the adolescent and sub-adult period. Finally, the recommendations were made for batteries of tests, which provided more comprehensive and efficient coverage of physical factors.

According to Cozen,[18] in his study "Strength test as measures of general athletic ability in college men", a weighted battery consists of the following individual tests:

Base-ball throw for distance, foot ball punt for distance, Bar snap for distance, standing broad jump, dodging or maze run, 300 yard run and dips were intercorrelated with Rogers strength test battery. Inter-correlation of all test items was calculated by the productive moment methods. Since the inter-correlation of all test items were calculated by the productive moment methods. The inter-correlation of General Athletic ability was computed from the data at hands, it seemed to coincide with the criteria. In computing multiple correlation coefficient and weight of Battery test items, when substitution for dips were made in the General Athletic ability test, Kelly's method of successive approximation was used. Using ten strength test items as criteria, a short battery of strength test was formulated. This Battery consists of five tests properly weighted Backlift, leg lift, arm push, chins, dips.

Barrow,[19] concluded a study to develop an easily administered test of motor ability for college men. Expert opinion was used in the validation process and eight factors of motor ability and 29 items measuring those factors were chosen. The selected tests were administered to 222 college men and statistical analysis covered by item reliability, objectivity, and correlation with the criteria and inter-correlations. Two test batteries including one short indoor test were recommended. Test scores should indicate performance in relation to norms, which have been established for the particular groups to be classified. Such norms were provided for both battery number one and battery number two for the following two groups: (a) for college men on an unclassified basis and (b) for physical education major students. The test's raw scores were recorded on a score card. By referring to the scoring table, the raw scores were converted into 'T' - scores and weighted standard scores. The weighted standard scores were summed and a general motor ability obtained. These scores were summed/referred to the appropriate table of norms and the students motor ability rating was found.

Gladys Scott. M,[20] in his study reveals that further development of test Battery. To compare additional measures of strength with the experimental battery and with work output comparison of test (pull, obstacle race, bounce sit-ups, chair-stepping) with work output. All these tests were administered in the same way as per the previous study except that chair stepping and sit-up were scored as total movement for one minute. This was based on recommendation from the previous study and later work with the tests. Work output was measured at maximum effort for one minute. This change was based on findings of a study by Tuttle and Wilson. Multiple correlation of various combinations of tests is computed and coefficient is given. Some three item combinations are approximately as good as four or five items. Similarly of coefficients for three, four, five items, combinations are largely the result of some relationship between the respective items. Conclusion of the study represents, no single items in the battery has a high enough relationship to work output to justify use of any single item. Each item has a significant relationship. The battery of four items has predictive value equal to that of five items battery. Pull test is the only test in the experimental battery with any relationship to the measures of the body size. There is some evidence that the pull test were refined to eliminate atleast a part of the advantage gained from weight.

Miller,[21] conducted a study on achievement level in basketball skills for women physical education majors. This study provides tables of norms in the form of T-scores and percentile rankings for raw scores made on three basketball skill tests—bounce and shoot, half-minute shoot, and pass for accuracy. Norms in the form of T-scores and percentile ranks have been determined based on the achievements of a very adequate number of subjects. It is expected that the tables of norms provided by this study will be of considerable aid to teachers in the professional physical education curriculum, in judging the adequacy of achievements of their students in basket ball skills, and will be of assistance to students in diagnosing their own strengths and weaknesses in this activity.

Mecloy,[22] established in his study, a factor analysis computed on 12 athletic events, administered to 400 men conditioned soldiers. Of these events, four could be considered to be test of circulo-respiratory endurance. Four were tests of muscular endurance and the other were tests of speed. In addition four combinations of tests were included. Four factors were found, one of circulo-respiratory endurance, one tentatively identified as mesomorphic body build. One important finding was a high factor weighting of the endurance index (300 yards run + 6 seconds run) with circulo-respiratory endurance (.8835). The purpose of the factorial analysis is to analyze the pure factors or components of which a given test is composed. That is the effort made to determine those pure factors, which are unrelated to each other.

Blair, Falls and Pate,[23] conducted a study on health-related physical fitness test. Percentile norms were developed by testing 12,000 children from age five to seventeen in Seventeen States. Tests excepting the skinfolds were administered in standardized manner by volunteer physical education teachers. Percentile norms for the skinfold tests were obtained from the national health examination survey. In an effort to assess the need for criterion referenced standard, recommendation for interpretation of test result had been included in the test manual.

According to Baugartner,[24] and his associates physical fitness was defined in this study as being muscular strength and endurance and cardio respiratory endurance. Thirteen fitness test items were administered to college women (N=336) and college men (N=283). Data were analyzed using four model and eight desired factor solutions. All the tests were administered over 2-week period. Test fatiguing similar muscle groups were not administered on the same day. The model utilized was incomplete principal component, alpa factor analysis, caronival factor analysis and incomplete image analysis. For each of the four initial solutions a derived orthogonal solutions was obtained by the Kaiser normal varimax procedure. The Harris-Kaiser orthoblique procedure with the positive manifold solution was used to secure oblique solutions. Conclusions of the study were the factors of physical fitness are not the same for college men and college women. For college men physical fitness as defined in this study has atleast three components, which is trunk strength and endurance. For college women physical fitness, as defined in this study, has three components, upper body strength and endurance, trunk strength and endurance and cardio respiratory endurance.

The AAHPERD Health-related fitness norms published in 1980 were based on over 12,000 boys and girls. A cluster sample representing several geographic regions was followed in 1985 and the results of national children and youth fitness study was published in the issue of Journal of Physical Education, Recreation and Dance. Over 8,500 boys and girls in grades five through 12 were administered health-related and motor fitness tests. This represents a national probability sample with few exceptions for selected age groups. The children that comprised the 1980 health-related physical fitness test sample were more fit than the 1985 Neyes Sample.[25]

Jackson,[26] in his study investigated the factor structure of the three factor strength model proposed by Fleishman. A theoretical model of nine hypothesized factors was developed and 25 tests sampled the hypothesized factors. The data collected on 76 college men were subjected to eight derived factor solutions. 25 tests were individually administered to the subject during seven different test sessions spread over a three month period. Four models of factor analysis were used to secure the initial solutions. The Harris Kaises orthoblique procedures were used to secure the oblique solutions. Based on the study the evidence presented in this analysis does not support the factors of dynamic strength, static strength and explosive strength reported by Fleishman. He reported that the common critical feature of the factor static strength is the required maximum force to be exerted for a brief period of time where the force that is exerted continuously goes upto the maximum, and this factor is generally to the arms and legs. However, the presented solutions of this study indicate that individual differences in muscular strength are a function of the arms and legs and that if the weight load is constant and sufficiently heavy, static and dynamic measures performed to exhaustion sample the same basic ability as test that requires a maximum force exerted over a period of time. This study agrees with investigators that the factor explosive strength is multidimensional. A major finding of this study is that different basic abilities or running exist.

Mervin,[27] and his associate defined physical fitness into four factors in this previous study, which are cited in this chapter. In this second study, 13 fitness items were administered to 109 college women and 97 college men. Data were analyzed using 8 derived factor solutions. This present study was proposed and conducted to serve as a partial replica of the initial study and to serve as comparative investigation of the component and tests of physical fitness. Six testing sessions were used to administer the 13 tests. As in the initial study, data were analyzed using four models and eight derived factor solutions. Findings of this study suggested for men test component are chin-up, pull-up, push-up, half hold sit-ups, legraises; standing broad jump, jump and reach; 12-minutes run, 880 - yard run. For college women, modified push-up, overhand straight arm hang, modified chin-ups; bent knee sit-up; standing broadjump; jump and reach, 50 yard dash, 12-minutes run.

According to Hapkins,[28] study, a theoretical model of the hypothesized dimensions of basket ball playing ability was developed based on a review literature concerning basketball skill testing from 1906 to the present day. These dimensions were (a) Shooting, (b) Passing, (c) Jumping, (d) Movement without the ball and (e) Movement with the ball. 21 items, including nine items in the AAHAPERD basketball skill test were administered to 70 male students in University of Minnesota. Hypothesized dimensions were analyzed basing on the four factor analysis. Both oblique and orthogonal rotation were performed with each of the four analyzes. The hypothesized model was partially substantiated in the results confirmed three of the factors (a) Shooting, (b) Passing and (c) Jumping with ball and without ball. Movement combined into one. Since the following test items best represented the dimensions, it appeared that a battery comprised of these items would provide a quick and objective measure of basket ball skill test (a) Jump and reach (b) Dribbling, (c) Speed run and (d) Front shot.

Powell,[29] and Eugene conducted a study on Newton motor ability test to establish adequate motor ability criteria and for the selection of tests which were valid, reliable, suitable and interesting to high school girls. Consideration was also given to the question of practicability and economy. Three motor ability criteria were established: (1) score based upon six sports skill tests, (2) score based upon a series of tests devised to measure various fundamental skills and various aspects of motor ability, (3) Subjective rating by jury of judges who observed the students while running obstacle race. Those scores on these tests were T-scores, and the average T-score was taken to be the sports criterion. The objective criterion of general motor ability was obtained from scores on eighteen objective tests each given twice. They noted that scramble, test of general ability, correlated more highly with the sports criterion than any other of the ten tests. They observed the jump and reach and the power and strength are important elements of athletic ability. The most important tests with respect to subjective rating of general motor ability were the hurdles and Broad jump. In relation to all three criteria, the broad jump and hurdles are clearly superior to the other tests. They recommended that for diagnostic purpose it might be desirable to use a four part motor ability test battery consisting of (1) Broad Jump, (2) Hurdles, (3) Scramble and (4) Velocity throw.

Connor and Cureton,[30] conducted a test on 660 high school girls to develop two motor fitness screen tests (1) A single period test of six items, (2) a double period test of twelve items. Their aim was to design period test of twelve items. Their aim was to design short, reliable and valid ways of screening the relatively unfit girls from those relatively more fit girls in motor fitness, to administer easily and quickly at indoors or out doors with little equipment. They have selected 19 test items and categorised these items into six specific aspects of fundamental body movements namely, Ability, Strength, Balance, Flexibility, Power and Endurance. In determining the validity of test items, the composite score of the items was selected of the criterion, as any one test seems to measure too narrow an area to adequately represent motor fitness. The valid coefficients are used to select the relatively more valid items and to eliminate those have very poor at round predictive value. Based these scores and calculations, they have selected six items for the six item test and eliminated 13 items. Further they selected six more items for the 12-item test this eliminating seven remaining tests. The items were selected into six categories of Balance flexibility, strength, ability, power and endurance. They recommended the 12-item test than the 6-item test if time permits.

Faine and Mathews,[31] in their study made an attempt to (a) apply suitable methods of testing physical fitness to mass investigational; (b) find "normal" values for the groups investigated and compare these with comparable figures obtained by other investigators; (c) Correlate the results obtained with other measures of health and scholastic achievement. They conducted the test on 125 school children to test physical fitness. Their testing procedure includes measuring resting pulse rate than undergoing a standard exercise followed by pulse rate after exercise. They observed that (1) maximal pulse rate after exercise, (2) The rate of declaration of the pulse are two chief factors that reflect the physiological condition in pulse rate tests. They also recommended that while the use of the two minute total pulse may be quite valid, the use of the changes that is the ratio gives a clearer picture of the changes that have taken place and may also enable a narrow range of normality to be defined.

Carpenter,[32] did a study on Johnson motor educability test, which consists often, items on 128 high school girls. Originally the Johnson test consists of 10 items but later Bartow and Roads included another 8 test items to that of Johnson type test making the total test items into 18. Scores were recorded from 128 school girls. The individuals test results were correlated with the total score for all eighteen and with the total score of original ten. Those tests which should lower correlation with the two criteria (nos.5-6) as well as those whose means were 50 high treat obviously the tests are too easy for high school level, were eliminated from further study. The remaining twelve tests, their total, the strength index and physical fitness index for each of the girls were inter-correlated and put into a factor analysis. The significance of results such as those obtained from a factor analysis is that one can pick out the specifically different things that are measured by the tests. In the process of factor analysis tests group themselves the ones testing a specific thing from a group showing test they measured this specific thing, or "factor", to a certain degree. The factor loading of each list is the correlation of the test with that factor.

Athchia Pillai,[33] conducted a study on computation of norms for 12-minute run and walk among school boys. In his study he described cardio-vascular endurance is one of the basic and important components of physical fitness, a state level norm will be useful for boys to understand their present status compared with other boys of the same age, for the teacher and coach either to understand or to prescribe a programme to improve the student ability and to compare it with other states. Since 15,000 subjects are involved in the study, 12-minutes walk test has been considered as the more appropriate test for assessing cardiovascular endurance.

For this study, data were collected from 20 districts except the Nilgiris district. Data collected from 250 subjects in each age category of 13, 14 and 15 years school boys. Tests were conducted on 12-minutes run/walk and the distance covered the nearest 50th metre were recorded as their performance.

Two-way analysis of variance was applied to find out whether there was any significant difference between the district and age group in 12-minutes run/walk performance. It was found that significant difference was noticed only among different age groups. Hence, norms were constructed throughout the state for different age groups by using Hull scale.

REFERENCES

1. Paul A. Hunsicker and Guy G.Reiff, AAHPERD Youth Fitness Test Manual; *Rev.ed. (Reston. Va: American alliance for Health and Physical Education, Recreation and Dance, 1976).*
2. Elizabeth G.Glover, "Physical Fitness test items in the first, second and Third grades". *Masters thesis, Women College, University of North Carolina, 1962.*
3. Arnett Chappelle, "The Purdue Motor Fitness Test Batteries for Senior High School Girls". *Research Quarterly, Vol.33, No.3, October 1962, p.323.*
4. Lawrence A.Holding and Andrew S.Jackson, "New National Norms 'Y' Way to Physical Fitness", *Journal of Physical Education, 78:4 (November/ December1980), pp.44-45.*

5. Lueien Brouha and M.V. Ball, Canadian Red Cross Society's Meal Study, *(Toronto; University of Toronto Press, 1952), p.55.*

6. Dale Mood, 'Test of Physical Fitness Knowledge Construction Administration and Norms: " *Research Quarterly, 42:1 (1971) p.423.*

7. AAHPHERD Health related physical fitness test manual Reston *(Va. American alliance for health, Physical Education, Recreation and Dance, 1980).*

8. AAHPERD Health Related Physical Fitness Technical Manual *(Reston Va; American Alliance for Health, Physical, Education, Recreation and Dance, 1984).*

9. Harold B.Falls, "AAHPERD Implements New Health/Fitness Test", *Physician and Sports Medicine, 8:6 (June 1979), p.27.*

10. Texas Governor Commission on Physical Fitness - Motor Ability tests, Texas Youth Fitness Test, *Austin, Texas, 1973, p.86.*

11. Lawry B.Fletcher, "The Relationship of Selected Factors to the Physical Fitness of Senior High School Boys in Arkanasa", *Journal of Physical Education, (1968), p.88.*

12. Agnes Wayman, "What to measure in Physical Education", *Research Quarterly, Vol.1, No.2, 1930; pp.98-99..*

13. Robson, "A simple Physical Fitness Test Battery for Elementary School Children", *SNIPES Journal, I:2, (April -1978), p.29.*

14. Victor C.Dunder, "A Multiple strength index of general motor ability", *Research Quarterly, Vol.4, No.3, 1936, pp.132-133.*

15. Henry J.Monotoye and Donald E. Lamphiear, 'Grip and Arm Strength in Males and Females, Age 10 to 69", *Research Quarterly, 48:1 (March 1977), p.109.*

16. Arthur J.Wendler, "A Critical analysis of test element used in Physical Education", *Research Quarterly, Vol.9, No: 1938; pp.64-76.*

17. Edwin A. Fleishman, "The Dimensions of Physical Fitness-the Nationwide Normative and Developmental study of Basic Tests", *Research Quarterly, 34:2 (May 1963), p.251.*

18. Frederick W.Cozen: 'Strength tests and measures of general Athletic ability in college men", *Research Quarterly, Vol.11, No.1, 1940; pp.45-52.*

19. Harold M. Barrow, 'Test of Motor Ability for College Men", *Research Quarterly, 25:3 (October, 1954), pp.253-260.*

20. Gladys Scott. M., 'Physical efficiency test for College Women", *Research Quarterly, Vol.19, No.1, 1948; pp.62-69.*

21. Wilma K.Miller, "Achievement Levels in Basket ball skills for Women Physical Education Major", *Research Quarterly, 25:4, (December 1954), pp.450-455.*

22. C.H.Mecloy, "A Factor Analysis of Test of Endurance", *Research Quarterly, Vol.27, No.1, 1956; p.213-216.*

23. Blair Steven N., Harold B. Falls and Russel R.Pate "A New Fitness Test", *The Physician and Sports Medicine, 11:4 (April 1983),* "A New Physical Fitness Test", *The Physician and Sports Medicine, p.94.*

24. A.Baumgartner and Marvin A.Zuidema, "Factor analysis of Physical Fitness Test", *Research Quarterly, Vol.43, No.4, 1972, pp.443-450.*

25. Author's Guide AAHPERD Health-related Physical Fitness Manual *as cited by Ted A.Baumgartner and Andrew S.Jackson Measurement for Evaluation in Physical Education and Exercise Science (3rd ed.) (Dubuque, IOWA: W.M.S. Brown Publishers, 1987), p.312.*

26. Andrew S.Jackson, "Factor Analysis of Selected Muscular Strength and Motor performance tests". *Research Quarterly, Vol.42, No.2, 1971, pp.164-172.*

27. Marvin A. Zuidema and Ted A.Baumgartner, "Second Factor Analysis study of Physical fitness tests", *Research Quarterly, Vol.45, No.3, 1974; pp.256-274.*

28. David R. Hopkins, "Factor Analysis of selected Basket Ball Skill Test", *Research Quarterly, Vol.48, No.3, 1977: pp.535-540.*

29. Elizabeth Powel and Eugene C. Home, "Motor ability tests for High School Girls", *Research Quarterly, Vol.10, No.4, (1939), p.81.*

30. Mary Evangeline or Cornor, Thomas Kirk Wraton, "Motor Fitness tests for high school girls", *Research Quarterly, Vol.16, (M, 1945), p.81.*

31. Solomon Faine, Devis T.Mathews. "Physical Fitness tests on Newzealand School Children", *Research Quarterly, Vol.22, (Dec. 1951), p.399.*

32. Allen Carpentar "Factors in Motor Educability" *Research quarterly, Vol.-14 (No.4-1943) p.366.*

33. Athicha Pillai, "Computation of norms for 12-minutes run and walk among school boys", *unpublished Doctoral thesis, Alagappa University, Karaikudi, 1991.*

CHAPTER—3

METHODOLOGY

In this chapter the selection of subjects, selection of variables, tester's reliability, test administration, collection of data and statistical techniques for construction of norms and to standardise the existing test items have been presented.

SELECTION OF SUBJECTS

The study was designed for construction of norms for the valid physical efficiency test for Physical Education Common Entrance Test in Andhra Pradesh. For this purpose the data has been collected from three regions of Andhra Pradesh i.e., Rayalaseema, Andhra, Telangana covering 23 districts (Figure 3.1) consist of 1050 male and 628 female students selected in random sample representing the same number from each district. The students who have attended for the physical efficiency test to seek admission into Bachelor of Physical Education (B.P.Ed) course in various colleges through the Physical Education Common Entrance Test (P.E.C.E.T) conducted by Government of Andhra Pradesh with a specific age group between 20 to 23 years of male and female students were taken as subject for the study.

SELECTION OF VARIABLES

All the test items which are present in the physical efficiency test of the Common Entrance Test were taken as variables for this study. The test items are:

MEN	*WOMEN*
1. 100 Mts. Run	1. 100 Mts. Run
2. 800 Mts. Run	2. 400 Mts. Run
3. High Jump	3. High Jump
4. Long Jump	4. Long Jump
5. Shot-put	5. Shot-put

TESTER'S RELIABILITY

As the testers were large in number and different persons worked as testers at different regions, the tester reliability could not be established.

However, all the testers were well qualified for the job and had rich experience in their respective fields. Moreover the day prior to the test administration an orientation session was conducted by the Convenor and regional observers to all the personnel involved in the testing and measuring procedures.

INSTRUMENT RELIABILITY

All the equipment and instruments used for the purpose of test administration were supplied by the Convenor and Regional Observers to the testers. All the equipment and the instruments were of high quality and were tested and re-tested before handing them over to the testers.

TEST ADMINISTRATION

Every candidate was supplied with a programme sheet well in advance and he/she has been directed to appear for the tests right on time.

The items tested were:

- 100 mts. run for men and women,

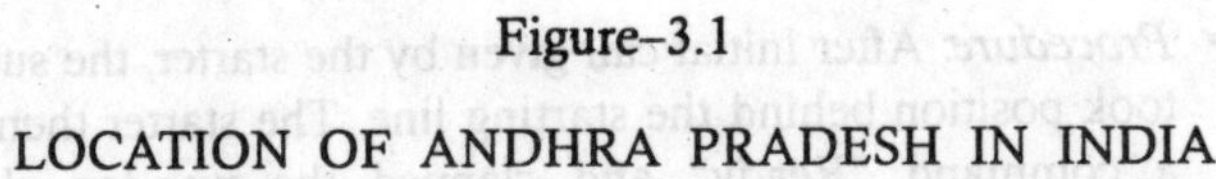

Figure–3.1
LOCATION OF ANDHRA PRADESH IN INDIA

- ➤ 800 Mts. run for men and 400 Mts. run for women,
- ➤ High jump for men and women,
- ➤ Long jump for men and women
- ➤ Shot put for men and women.

100 Mts. Run for Men and Women

- *Purpose*: To measure speed.
- *Facilities and Equipment*: Standard track with eight lanes, Eight stop watches, one Ten-memory split second timer, one clap board.

- *Procedure*: After initial call given by the starter, the subjects took position behind the starting line. The starter then gave a command "Ready" and clapped the wooden clapper indicating the subjects "to go". The subjects ran across the finish line. Only one trail is permitted. Subjects were permitted to take "crouch" start.
- *Testing Personnel*: One starter to start the race and his assistant positioned at the starting point. Eight timekeepers with stop watches to record the timing of the subject in their respective lanes. One person with a ten- memory timer to record all the eight timings to check with other timings so that there may not be much variations.
- *Scoring*: The score is the elapsed time to the nearest hundredth of a second between the starting signal and the instant the subject crosses the finish line.

800 Mts. Run for Men

- *Purpose*: To measure endurance.
- *Facilities and Equipment*: 400 mts. track with eight lanes.
- *Procedure*: Ten candidates run at a time. A curve was drawn in the starting line and the starter gave the command 'Ready' 'go'. The subjects ran two laps around the track and were free to run in first lane.
- *Testing personnel*: One starter, ten time keepers and one additional time keeper with a ten-memory timer, four lane judges to prevent the subjects from cutting into the inside of the track.
- *Scoring*: Time elapsed to complete the race was recorded in minutes and seconds.

400 Mts. Run for Women

- *Purpose*: To measure endurance.
- *Facilities and Equipment*: 400 mts. track with eight lanes.
- *Procedure*: Eight candidates run at a time. The starter gave the command "Ready" 'go'. The subjects ran one lap around the track on their own lanes.

- *Testing personnel*: One starter, eight time keeper with a ten-memory timer, four lane judges to prevent the subjects from cutting into the inside of the track and other lanes.
- *Scoring*: Time elapsed to complete the race was recorded in minutes and seconds.

High Jump for Men and Women

- *Purpose*: To measure the explosive strength on legs.
- *Facilities*: High-jump up-rights, with cross bar and jumping pit.
- *Procedure*: The minimum height of the bar for men was 3' 6" and for women 2' 6". Further the ball was raised 2 inches each time. The test was conducted by following I.A.A.F. rules i.e., three consecutive failures keep the subject out of competition.
- *Testing personnel*: Two persons to adjust the cross bar, one person to call the number.
- *Scoring*: Maximum height cleared by the individual was recorded in feet and inches and converted into metres for calculation purpose.

Long Jump for Men and Women

- *Purpose*: To measure the explosive strength of legs.
- *Facilities and Equipment*: Standard long jump pit and take-off board, measuring tape.
- *Procedure*: When the subjects numbers were called, they took position in the runway, ran to the take off board and jumped into the pit. Three trials were given for each subject and best will be considered.
- *Testing personnel*: One person to call the numbers, two persons to measure the distance and one person to call "foul" if committed by any subject.
- *Scoring*: The distance between the take-off line and the nearest point where any part of the subject's body touches the floor (Jumping-pit), it was measured in feet and inches to the nearest inches. The data was converted to metres for calculation purpose.

Shot Put for Men and Women

- *Purpose*: To measure explosive strength of arm and shoulder gridle.
- *Facilities and Equipment*: Shot put circle and sector, 12 lbs. shot for men 8 lbs. shot for women and measuring tape.
- *Procedure*: Each subject was given three chances to put the shot into the sector.
- *Testing personnel*: Two persons for measuring, one person for calling the number and to jude the fouls.
- *Scoring*: Distance between the circle line and the nearest point where the shot landed on the ground. The tape will be placed in the centre of the circle, but the recording will be taken only upto the inner edge of the Toe boards. Scores were recorded in meters and centimeters.

The above test procedures were followed by the conveners of PECET. The data was collected from the records of the conveners for the purpose of the present study.

STANDARDS IN CONSTRUCTING NORMS

The procedure for construction of norms to standardise the test item starts with the collection of scores on the test from a large sample of students from the population for which the test is intended. To be accepted as valid and practical criteria the Norm scales and Standardizing test items are to be constructed with practical, statistical and educational principles.

Clarke[1], has suggested the following factors to evaluate the norm chart :

1. Sampling procedure for the construction of norms should be based upon wide distribution of the population.
2. Testing sample should be representative of the population for which the test is intended.
3. Norms should be used for the specific groups for which they are prepared.
4. Norms should be used for the specific groups standard tests should be based upon a relatively large number of cases.

Norms represent the achievement level of a particular group to which obtained scores can be compared. In a table of Norms raw scores and derived scores are typically presented in parallel columns for easy conversion to derive scores. It is obvious that test accompanied by norms has several advantages over tests without norms. Norms enable the instructor to interpret student scores in relation to a large group in the same population. Their use enables a comparison of the performance of a student with other pupil and gives uniform meaning to the comparison of students scores on one test with his or her scores on another. In addition norms provides a reliable and useful basis for interpretation and evaluation of test results.

STATISTICAL PROCEDURE

To fulfil our objectives it is proposed to consider the 'Multiple linear regression analysis'[2] in the present study. This analysis has been carried out separately for men and women. In each category five major variables were identified to determine the criterion score. Hence, the functional relationship was established between criterion score and the selected five independent variables. The proposed functional form is

$$y = f(x_1, x_2, x_3, x_4, x_5)$$

Specifically the multiple linear regression for men is

$$y = a_0 + a_1x_1 + a_2x_2 + a_3x_3 + a_4x_4 + a_5x_5$$

where y = criterion score

x_1 = 100 Mts. run

x_2 = 800 Mts. run

x_3 = High Jump

x_4 = Long Jump

x_5 = Shot Put$_1$,

a_1, a_2, a_3, a_4, a_5 are the estimated coefficients of the variable and ao is the intercept term.

To test the significance of each independent variable on criterion score, t-test statistic has been carried out. To determine the combined effect of all variables on criterion score, the multiple correlation coefficient R^2 was calculated and for its significance, F-test statistic has been computed.

In the present study, to establish the new norms for independent variables, it is proposed to estimate the two other regression models wise

$$Y = f(x_1, x_2, x_4, x_5) \text{ and}$$

$$Y = f(x_1, x_2, x_3, x_5)$$

Similarly in the case of women candidates, the study is also proposed to estimate the regression model with the same variables except x_2 variable (Instead of 800mts. 400mts. was considered). The proposed model is

$Y = f(x_1, x_2, x_3, x_4, x_5)$ specifically the model in the form

$$Y = bo + b_1x_1 + b_2x_2 + b_3x_3 + b_4x_4 + b_5x_5$$

where Y = criterion score

x_1 = 100 Mts. run

x_2 = 400 Mts. run

x_3 = High Jump

x_4 = Long Jump

x_5 = Shot Put.

where b_1, b_2, b_3, b_4, b_5 are the estimated regression coefficient of the corresponding variables and b_0 is the intercept term.

To highlight the net effect of x_3 and x_4 variables on dependent variables, two other functional relationships were formulated.

$$y = f(x_1, x_2, x_4, x_5)$$

$$y = f(x_1, x_2, x_3, x_5)$$

The analysis and the results were drawn according to the estimated coefficients.

To study the relationship between each independent variable, correlation matrix was calculated. From this 'correlation matrix'[3] one can say how best the each independent variable is correlated with the set of other independent variables. The percentage of relations and their direction of (positive or negative) relation were explained.

For construction of norms "Hull Scale"[4] statistical techniques were applied by fixing point scale from 1-100. Norms indicate a students relative position in a group. The Hull Scale which extends 3.5 sigmas on either side of the mean was utilized to construct the norms, Since it goes beyond the somewhat narrow limits of the 6-sigma scale and it does not leave the ends of the scale like T-scale.

REFERENCES

1. Harrison Clarke, "Application of Measurement to Health and Physical Education", *(5th ed.)(Englewood Cliffs, New Jercy : Prentice Hall Inc. 1976) p.30.*
2. S. C. Gupta and V. K. Kapoor, "Fundamentals of Applied Statistics", *Sultan Chand & Sons, 3rd ed., 1994, p. 8.1-8.36*
3. Paul Bewbold, "Statistics for Business and Economics", *Prentice Hall International, 2nd ed., 1988, pp. 488-650.*
4. D.Allen Philips and James E. Hornak. " Measurement and Evaluation in Physical Education", *ed. John Willey and sons, Inc., New York, 1976, pp. 91-92.*

CHAPTER—4

ANALYSIS OF DATA AND DISCUSSION OF THE STUDY

In this chapter the statistical analysis of the data collected have been presented. For the purpose of the study, data were collected from 1050 men and 628 women candidates (Appendix-I & II), who attended the Physical Education Common Entrance Test (PECET) in Andhra Pradesh. To standardize the test items and to construct the norms for test the data was selected from the candidates who obtained the minimum of 30 percent score in aggregate out of five variables. The raw scores are converted to standard scores by using present conversion score norms (Appendix-V & VI). Further, the samples are reduced to 851 men and 499 women candidates (Appendix-III & IV).

The aim of the study was to find out the association of independent variables i.e., 100 Mts. Run, 800 Mts. run, High Jump, Long Jump and Shot Put for men and 100 Mts. run, 400 Mts. run, High Jump, Long Jump and Shot Put for women with criterion variable (some of the scores of five variables) to standardize and to fix test items for physical efficiency test. Further the study is extended to construct the new norms for the test items.

For the purpose of the study to find out the association of independent variables with criterion variable the statistical technique *"Multiple linear regression analysis"* was applied. For construction of norms *"Hull Scale"* statistical technique was applied by fixing the point scale from 1-100.

In this chapter the study was discussed in four separate heads. They are Regression analysis on men test, Regression analysis on women test, Construction of norms for men test and Construction of norms for women test.

REGRESSION ANALYSIS OF PHYSICAL EFFICIENCY TEST ITEMS

Men Test : All Variables Considered

Regression Analysis:

To establish the functional relationship between criterion score (Y) and the remaining independent variables 100 Mts. (X_1) 800 Mts. (X_2) High Jump (X_3), Long Jump (X_4) and Shot Put (X_5), it is proposed to fit the multiple linear regression model of the form,

$$Y = a_o + a_1 x_1 + a_2 x_2 + a_3 x_3 + a_4 x_4 + a_5 x_5$$

The collected data relating to the variables in the present study fed with the regression model and results are given in the Table-4.1.

The estimated regression equation is

$$Y = 180.536 - \underset{(0.163)}{5.252^{*}} X1 + \underset{(0.069)}{1.135^{*}} x2 + \underset{(0.102)}{1.411^{*}} X3 + \underset{(0.156)}{4.046^{*}} X4 + \underset{(0.283)}{2.171^{*}} X5$$

$R^2 = 2.064$ $R^2 = 2.071$

$D = 1.935$ $F = 327.80^{*}$

* Significant at 5 percent probability level.

Figures in the parenthesis are the standard errors of the estimates.

TABLE–4.1
REGRESSION ANALYSIS OF MEN TEST WITH ALL 5 VARIABLES

Variable	*Slope*	*Mean*	*S.E.E.*	*t-value*	*S.D.*
100m (x_1)	–5.252	61.779	0.163	–32.153	13.207
800m (x_2)	1.135	20.200	0.069	16.329	25.172
High Jump (x_3)	1.411	46.895	0.102	13.877	18.563
Long Jump (x_4)	4.046	42.974	0.156	25.975	13.990
Shot Put (x_5)	2.171	44.095	0.283	7.679	6.398
Criterion (Y)		224.944			47.814
(Intercept)	180.536				

CORRELATION MATRIX

Variables	*100m*	*800m*	*High*	*Long*	*Shot*
100m	[1.000	0.172	0.361	0.583	0.255]
800m	[	1.000	–0.019	0.128	–0.089]
High	[		1.000	0.387	0.215]
Long	[			1.000	0.287]
Shot	[				1.000]

R (squared) = 2.064 Rbar (squared) = 2.071

D Statistic = 1.935

ANALYSIS OF VARIANCE

Source	*D.F.*	*Sum of Squares*	*Mean of Squares*	*F value*
Due to regression within groups	5	4016089.750	803217.938	–327.80
Due to residuals	845	–2070519.500	–2450.319	
Total	850	1945570.250		

The estimated regression co-efficient of all independent variables except X_1 (100mt) shows positive and significant effect on criterion score (Y).

The coefficient of X_1 is negative and significant. It means an increase in one unit in X_1 variable will decrease the criterion score by 5.25 units. It represents the negative relationship with criterion score. The negative and significant value reveals that there is a scope to increase the standards and norms of Y by standardising the norms in X_1 variable. The estimated coefficients of X_2, X_3, X_4 and X_5 variable shows positive relationship with the criterion score individually. An increase in one unit of each and above four variables will increase the criterion score by 1.135, 1.411, 4.046 and 2.171 units respectively. This positive relationship is significant at 5 percent probability level on criterion score. The value of constant and intercept is 180.536, which expresses the effect of variables, which are not considered in the model.

The collective effect of all explanatory variables on explained variable is called as multiple correlation co-efficient. It is denoted by R^2. The adjusted multiple correlation coefficient $\bar{R}^2$ is also carried out. The value of R^2 is 2.064. To test the collective effect of all explanatory variables on Y, F-test statistic has been computed.The estimated value of F is 327.80. From F-test statistic, it is inferred that the F-value is significant at 5 percent probability level.D-statistic represents the serial-correlation or auto-correlation, it means the correlation between observations in the variable.The estimated D statistic is 1.935, expresses that there is no serial-correlation in the data.

CORRELATION ANALYSIS

The estimated correlation matrix shows inter relationship in explanatory variables. It explains how best one dependent variable related to the set of independent variables. It is shown in the form of correlation matrix.

The correlation co-efficients are as follows:

100 Mts., 800 Mts. run is	0.172	=	17.2 percent
100 Mts. High Jump is	0.361	=	36.1 percent
100 Mts. Long Jump is	0.583	=	58.3 percent
100 Mts. Shot Put is	0.255	=	25.5 percent
800 Mts. High Jump is -0.019		=	- 2 percent

800 Mts. Long Jump is	0.128	=	12.8 percent
800 Mts. Shot Put is	0.089	=	- 9 percent
High Jump, Long Jump is	0.387	=	38.7 percent
High Jump, Long Jump is	0.215	=	21.5 percent
Long Jump, Shot Put is	0.287	=	28.7 percent

Negative correlated items are:

800 Mts. High Jump	2 percent
800 Mts. Shot Put	9 percent

From the correlation matrix it is observed that the High Jump variable shows negative relationship with 800 mts. variable. It shows positive relationship with 100 mts. and Shot put variable. The High Jump and Long-Jump variables are having the positive correlation (38.7%) with each other. In the case of Long-Jump variables, positive relationship was observed with all explanatory variables. The relation between Shot Put and 800 Mts. is negative (-9%), whereas the other variables relationship with Shot Put variable is positive. 100 Mts. run having positive association with other variables independently. The 800 Mts. run shows negative relationship with High Jump variable.

Men Test: Dropping of the High Jump Variable

In the second model the functional relationship was established on explained variable Y by all the explanatory variables, excluding the variable High Jump (X_3), therefore, the estimated model is of the form,

$$Y = a_o + a_1 x_1 + a_2 x_2 + a_4 x_4 + a_5 x_5$$

The collected data relating to the variable in the present study was fed with the regression model and results are given in the Table 4.2

The estimated regression equation is

$$\begin{array}{l} \qquad\qquad\qquad\qquad * \qquad\qquad * \qquad\qquad * \qquad\qquad * \\ Y = 188.610 - 4.844 \text{ x1} + 1.052 \text{ x2} + 4.521 \text{ X4} + 2.508 \text{ X5} \\ \qquad\qquad\qquad (0.141) \qquad (0.061) \qquad (0.133) \qquad (0.247) \end{array}$$

$R^2 = 1.822$ $\qquad$ $R^{-2} = 1.826$

D = 1.760 F = 468.89*

* Significant at 5 percent probability level.

Figures in the parenthesis are the standard errors of the estimate.

TABLE-4.2

REGRESSION ANALYSIS OF MEN TEST BY DROPPING HIGH JUMP VARIABLE

Variable		*Slope*	*Mean*	*S.E.E.*	*t-value*	*S.D.*
100m	(x_1)	–4.844	61.779	0.141	–34.329	13.207
800m	(x_2)	1.052	29.200	0.061	17.302	25.172
Long Jump	(x_4)	4.521	42.974	0.133	33.880	13.990
Shot Put	(x_5)	2.508	44.095	0.247	10.140	6.398
Criterion	(Y)		224.944			47.814
(Intercept)		188.610				

CORRELATION MATRIX

Variables	*100m*	*800m*	*Long*	*Shot*
100m	[1.000	0.172	0.583	0.255]
800m	[	1.000	0.128	–0.089]
Long	[		1.000	0.287]
Shot	[			1.000]

R (squared) = 1.822 Rbar (squared) = 1.826

D Statistic = 1.760

ANALYSIS OF VARIANCE

Source	*D.F.*	*Sum of Squares*	*Mean of Squares*	*F value*
Due to regression within groups	4	3544252.0000	886063.000	–468.89
Due to residuals	846	–1598681.750	–1889.695	
Total	850	1945570.250		

The estimated regression co-efficients of all independent variables except X_1 (100mt) shows the positive and significant effect on criterion score (Y).

The co-efficient of X_1 is negative and significant. It represents the negative relationship with criterion score variable. It means, an increase in one unit in X_1 variable will decrease the criterion score by 4.84 units. The negative and significant value reveals that there is a scope to increase the standards and norms of Y by increasing the standards in X_1 variable. The estimated coefficients of X_2, X_4 and X_5 variables show positive relationship with the criterion score individually. An increase in one unit of each and above three variables will increase the criterion score by 1.052, 4.521 and 2.508 units respectively. This positive relationship is significant at 5 percent probability level on criterion score. The value of intercept term is 188.610.

The multiple correlation coefficient R^2 is 1.822. To test the collective effect of all variables on Y, F- test statistic has been computed. The estimated value of F is 468.89. The value of 'F' is significant at 5 percent probability level. The estimated D-statistic value is 1.760, it expresses that there is no serial-correlation in the data.

By dropping the High Jump (X_3) from the first model the collective effect of the variables (X_1, X_2, X_4 and X_5) on criterion score (Y) decrease 0.232 units. It shows that the net effect of High Jump (X_3) variable on Y is 0.232 units. Hence, it is inferred that the dropping of X_3 variable will decrease the 23 percent in total relationship with the criterion score Y.

The dropping of high jump variable resulted

41 percent increase in weightage for 100 Mts. score

8 percent decrease in weightage for 800 Mts. score

47.5 percent increase in weightage for long-jump score

33.7 percent increase in weightage of shot-put score.

The total variation in criterion score was decreased by 12 percent was observed by dropping the High Jump variable over the first model.

Men Test: Dropping of the Long-Jump Variable

To establish the functional relationship between criterion scores (Y) and the independent variables 100 Mts. (X_1), 800 Mts. (X_2) High Jump (X_3) and Shot Put (X_5) after dropping Long Jump variable (X_4), it is proposed to fit the multiple linear regression model of the form.

$$Y = a_o + a_1x_1 + a_2x_2 + a_3x_3 + a_5x_5$$

The collected data relating to the variables in the model given above was fed with the regression model and results are given in the Table–4.3

The estimated regression equation is

$$Y = 147.272 - \underset{(0.065)}{3.238^{*}}\, X_1 + \underset{(0.031)}{1.276^{*}}\, X_2 + \underset{(0.045)}{1.992^{*}}\, X_3 + \underset{(0.125)}{3.335^{*}}\, X_5$$

$R^2 = 1.215$ $\qquad \bar{R}^2 = 1.216$

$D = 1.509$ $\qquad F = 1197.51^{*}$

* Significant at 5 percent probability level.

Figures in the parenthesis are the standard errors of the estimates.

The estimated regression co-efficient of independent variables except X_1 (100mt) shows positive and significant effect on criterion score (Y).

TABLE–4.3

REGRESSION ANALYSIS OF MEN TEST BY DROPPING LONG JUMP VARIABLE

Variable		*Slope*	*Mean*	*S.E.E.*	*t-value*	*S.D.*
100m	(x_1)	–3.238	61.779	0.065	–50.197	13.207
800m	(x_2)	1.276	29.200	0.031	41.056	25.172
High Jump	(x_3)	1.992	46.895	0.045	44.749	18.563
Shot Put	(x_5)	3.335	44.095	0.125	26.628	6.398
Criterion	(Y)		224.944			47.814
(Intercept)		147.272				

CORRELATION MATRIX

Variables	*100m*	*800m*	*High*	*Shot*
100m	[1.000	0.172	0.361	0.255]
800m	[	1.000	–0.019	–0.089]
High	[		1.000	0.215]
Shot	[			1.000]

R (squared) = 1.215 Rbar (squared) = 1.216
D Statistic = 1.509

ANALYSIS OF VARIANCE

Source	*D.F.*	*Sum of Squares*	*Mean of Squares*	*F value*
Due to regression within groups	4	2362897.250	590724.313	–1197.51
Due to residuals	846	–417327.000	–493.294	
Total	850	1945570.250		

The coefficient of X_1 is negative and significant, it means an increase in one unit in X_1 variable will decrease the criterion score by 3.24 units. It represents the negative relationship with criterion score. The estimated coefficients of X_2, X_3 and X_5 variables show positive and significant relationship with the criterion score individually. An increase in one unit of each and above variables X_2, X_3, X_5 willincrease the criterion score by 1.276, 1.992 and 3.335 units respectively. This positive relationship is significant at 5 percent probability level on criterion score. The constant and intercept term value is 147.272.

The collective effect of all explanatory variables on the explained variable (R^2) is 1.215. To test this collective effect of all variables on Y, F - test statistic was computed. The estimated value of F is 1197.51 and it is significant at 5 percent probability level. Durbin and Watson, D-Statistic was estimated and it is 1.509, it expresses that there is no serial-correlation in the data.

Comparing the values of R^2 in the models one and three, it is observed that there is some decrease i.e., 0.849 units nearly 42 percent over the first model. Hence it is inferred that the dropping of Long Jump variable from the model decreases the collective effect on criterion score.

Dropping of Long Jump variable result the significant increase in the effect of all variables on criterion score. Specifically

200 percent increase in weightages for 100 Mts. score,

14 percent increase in weightage for 800 Mts. score,

58 percent increase in weightage for High Jump score

126 percent increase in weightage of Shot Put score.

The total variation in criterion scores was decreased by 41.1 percent was observed by dropping of Long Jump variable over the first model.

Women Test: All Variables Considered

Regression Analysis

In the case of women candidates, the relationship between Criterion score (Y) and the explanatory variables 100 Mts. (X_1) 400 Mts. (X_2) High Jump (X_3) Long Jump (X_4) and Shot Put (X_5) was established by applying multiple linear regression model of the Form.

$$Y = b_o + b_1 x_1 + b_2 x_2 + b_3 x_3 + b_4 x_4 + b_5 x_5$$

The intercept and regression coefficients of the Variables in the above specified model were estimated by using Ordinary least square method. The collected data was fed with the multiple linear regression models and the estimated results are given in the Table 4.4

The estimated regression equation is

$$Y = 600.258 + \underset{(0.191)}{0.174\,X1} - \underset{(0.243)}{5.641^{*}\,X2} + \underset{(0.177)}{0.508^{*}\,X3} +$$

$$\underset{(0.307)}{1.756^{*}\,X4} + \underset{(0.702)}{2.587^{*}\,X5}$$

$R^2 = 3.598$ $\bar{R}^2 = 3.625$

$D = 1.196$ $F = 136.55^{*}$

* Significant at 5 percent probability level.

Figures in the parenthesis are the standard errors of the estimates

The estimated regression co-efficients of all independent variables except X_2 (400 mts.) shows positive and significant effect on criterion score (Y).

TABLE–4.4

REGRESSION ANALYSIS OF WOMEN TEST WITH ALL 5 VARIABLES

Variable		*Slope*	*Mean*	*S.E.E.*	*t-value*	*S.D.*
100m	(x_1)	0.174	42.782	0.191	0.911	21.493
400m	(x_2)	–5.641	92.894	0.243	–23.190	13.486
High Jump	(x_3)	0.508	48.673	0.177	2.878	19.578
Long Jump	(x_4)	1.756	32.629	0.307	5.728	12.994
Shot Put	(x_5)	2.587	32.315	0.702	3.683	5.214
Criterion	(Y)		249.293			44.639
(Intercept)		600.258				

CORRELATION MATRIX

Variables	*100m*	*800m*	*High*	*Long*	*Shot*
100m	[1.000	–0.000	0.318	0.539	0.399]
400m	[	1.000	–0.138	0.023	0.042]
High	[		1.000	0.165	0.152]
Long	[			1.000	0.414]
Shot	[				1.000]

R (squared) = 3.598Rbar (squared) = 3.625

D Statistic = 1.196

ANALYSIS OF VARIANCE

Source	*D.F.*	*Sum of Squares*	*Mean of Squares*	*F value*
Due to regression within groups	5	3578006.500	715601.313	–136.55
Due to residuals	493	–2583696.188	–5240.763	
Total	498	994310.313		

The co-efficient of X_2 is negative and significan. it means an increase in one unit of X_2 will decrease the criterion score by 5.64 units. It represents the negative relationship with criterion score. The negative and significant value reveals that there is a scope to increase the criterion score value by standardizing the norms of X_2 variable. The estimated co-efficient of X_1, X_3, X_4 and X_5 variable shows positive relationship with the criterion score individually. This positive relationship with Y value is significant in the cases of X_3, X_4 and X_5 variables only. In the case of X_1 variable, the relationship with Y is not significant. An increase in one unit of each and above four variables will increase the criteria score by 0.174, 0.508, 1.756 and 2.587 units (X_1, X_3, X_4 and X_5)respectively. The value of constant and intercept term in the model is 600.258. It expresses, the effect of other variables, which are not considered in the model, on the explained variable (Y).

The combined effect of all explanatory variables on explained variable is called multiple correlation coefficient, it is denoted by R^2. The adjusted multiple correlation co-efficient $\overline{R}^2$ is also carried out and it is 3.625. The value of R^2 is 3.598.

The estimated value of F is 136.55. From F-test statistic, it is inferred that F-Value is significant at 5 percent probability level. It is inferred that the collective of all variables (x_i) in the model on Y is significant. D-statistic value is 1.196, indicates there is no series-correlation.

CORRELATION ANALYSIS

The estimated correlation matrix shows inter-relationship among explanatory variables. It explains how best one independent variable related to the set of other independent variables. It is shown in the form of correlation matrix.

The correlation co-efficients are as follows:

100 Mts. 400 Mts. is	–0	=	0.0 percent
100 Mts. High Jump is	0.318	=	31.8 percent
100 Mts. Long Jump is	0.539	=	53.9 percent
100 Mts. Shot Put is	0.339	=	33.9 percent
400 Mts. High Jump is	–0.138	=	–13.8 percent

400 Mts. Long Jump is	0.023	=	2.3 percent
400 Mts. Shot Put is	0.042	=	4.2 percent
High Jump, Long Jump is	0.165	=	16.5 percent
High Jump, Shot Put is	0.152	=	15.2 percent
Long Jump, Shot Put is	0.414	=	41.4 percent

Negative correlation items are

100 Mts. 400 Mts. is		=	0.0 percent
400 Mts. High Jump is		=	13.8 percent

From the correlation matrix it is observed that the 400 Mts. variable shows negative relationship with the 100 Mts. and high jump variable. It shows positive relation with Long Jump and Shot Put. The High Jump and Long Jump variable have the positive correlation (16.5%) with each other. In the case of Long Jump variable, positive relationship was observed with all explanatory variables. The relation between Shot Put and other variable is positive. 100 Mts. run having positive association with High Jump, Long Jump and Shot Put variables, negative relation with 400 Mts. run. The 400 Mts. run shown negative relation with High Jump variable and positive relation with Long Jump and Shot Put.

Women Test: Dropping of the High-Jump Variable

In the second model High Jump (X_3) variable was dropped from the previous model. Hence, the relationship was established between criterion score (Y) and the independent variables 100 Mts. (X_1), 400 Mts. (X_2) Long Jump (X_4) and Shotput (X_5). The proposed multiple linear regression model is of the form.

$$Y = b_o + b_1x_1 + b_2x_2 + b_4x_4 + b_5x_5.$$

The estimated regression coefficients along with their standard errors are shown in the Table-4.5

The estimated regression equation is

$$Y = 626.320 + \overset{**}{0.317}\underset{(0.182)}{X_1} - \overset{*}{5.744}\underset{(0.238)}{X_2} + \overset{*}{1.743}\underset{(0.304)}{X_4} + \overset{*}{2.665}\underset{(0.695)}{X_5}$$

$R^2 = 3.555$ $\bar{R}^2 = 3.576$

$D = 1.174$ $F = 171.84^*$

* Significant at 5 percent probability level.

** Significant at 10 percent probability level.

Figures in the parenthesis are the standard errors of the estimates.

The estimated coefficient of all independent variable except X_2 (400mt) shows the positive and significant effect on the criterion score (Y).

The co-efficient of X_2 is negative and significant. The estimated coefficient of X_1, X_4 and X_5 variable shows positive relationship with the criteria score individually. An increase in one unit of each and above 3 variable (X_1, X_4, X_5) will increase the criterion score by 0.317, 1.743 and 2.665 respectively. This positive relationship is significant at 5 percent probability level on criterion score. In the case of X_1 variable, it is observed that there is a positive and significant relationship at 10 percent probability level. The constant and intercept term value is 626.32. The estimated multiple correlation coefficient R^2 in 3.555. The adjusted multiple correlation was calculated and it is 3.576. Estimated F-Value is 171.84. F- value is significant at 5 percent probability level. It expresses that the multiple correlation with Y is significant. D-statistic value is 1.174. It may be observe that there is no serial-correlation in the variable. Exclusion of High Jump (X_3) variable from the model cannot shown any significant changes in the effects of the variable X_1, X_2, X_4 and X_5 on criterion score. From the values of R^2 in both the model, one can observed that there is some decrease in the second model i.e., 4.3 percent. The exclusion of X_3 variable never shows any significant decrease in the collective effect on Y.

The dropping of High Jump variable resulted in

14 percent increase in weightage for 100 Mts. score

10 percent decrease in weightage for 400 Mts. score

1 percent decrease in weightage for Long Jump score

8 percent increase in weightage for Shot Put score

TABLE–4.5

REGRESSION ANALYSIS OF WOMEN TEST BY DROPPING HIGH JUMP VARIABLE

Variable		*Slope*	*Mean*	*S.E.E.*	*t-value*	*S.D.*
100m	(x_1)	0.317	42.782	0.182	1.742	21.493
400m	(x_2)	–5.744	92.894	0.238	–24.102	13.486
Long Jump	(x_4)	1.743	32.629	0.304	5.742	12.994
Shot Put	(x_5)	2.665	32.315	0.695	3.833	5.214
Criterion	(Y)		249.293			44.639
(Intercept)		626.320				

CORRELATION MATRIX

Variables	*100m*	*400m*	*Long*	*Shot*
100m	[1.000	–0.000	0.539	0.399]
400m	[	1.000	0.023	0.042]
Long	[		1.000	0.414]
Shot	[			1.000]

R (squared) = 3.555 Rbar (squared) = 3.576

D Statistic = 1.174

ANALYSIS OF VARIANCE

Source	*D.F.*	*Sum of Squares*	*Mean of Squares*	*F value*
Due to regression within groups	4	3534612.250	883653.062	–171.84
Due to residuals	494	–2540301.938	–5142.312	
Total	498	994310.313		

The total variation in criterion score were decreased by 1.2 percent was observed by dropping the High Jump variable over the first model.

Women Test: Dropping of Long Jump Variable:

In the third model, the multiple linear regression equation is calculated by dropping long-jump (X_4) from the first model. The functional relationship between the criterion score (Y) and the remaining independent variables 100mt (X_1) 400 mts. (X_2) High Jump (X_3) and Shot Put (X_5) is given in the form.

$$Y = b_0 + b_1x_1 + b_2x_2 + b_3x_3 + b_5x_5$$

The collected data relating to the variables was fed in the regression model and results are given in the Table - 4.6

The estimated regression equation is

$$Y : 602.657 + \overset{*}{0.650}\, X_1 - \overset{*}{5.622}\, X_2 + \overset{*}{0.494}\, X_3 + \overset{*}{3.620}\, X_5$$
$$(0.166) \quad (0.235) \quad (0.170) \quad (0.655)$$

R^2 : 3.426 $\quad\quad \bar{R}^2$: 3.445

D : 1.176 $\quad\quad$ F : 174.42*

* Significant at 5 percent probability level.

Figures in the parenthesis are the standard errors of the estimates.

TABLE–4.6

REGRESSION ANALYSIS OF WOMEN TEST BY DROPPING LONG JUMP VARIABLE

Variable		*Slope*	*Mean*	*S.E.E.*	*t-value*	*S.D.*
100m	(x_1)	0.650	42.782	0.166	3.927	21.493
800m	(x_2)	–5.622	92.894	0.235	–23.946	13.486
High Jump	(x_3)	0.494	48.673	0.170	2.897	19.578
Shot Put	(x_5)	3.620	32.315	0.655	5.525	5.214
Criterion	(Y)		249.293			44.639
(Intercept)		602.657				

CORRELATION MATRIX

Variables	*100m*	*800m*	*High*	*Shot*
100m	[1.000	-0.000	0.318	0.399]
800m	[	1.000	-0.138	0.042]
High	[		1.000	0.152]
Shot	[			1.000]

R (squared)= 3.426Rbar (squared) = 3.445

D Statistic = 1.176

ANALYSIS OF VARIANCE

Source	*D.F.*	*Sum of Squares*	*Mean of Squares*	*F value*
Due to regression within groups	4	3406069.750	851517.438	-174.42
Due to residuals	494	-2411759.438	-4882.104	
Total	498	994310.313		

The estimated regression co-efficients of all independent variables except X_2 (400mt) shows positive and significant effect on criterion score (Y).

The co-efficient of X_2 is negative and significant. It represents the negative relationship with criterion score. It means an increase in one unit of X_2 variable will decrease the criterion score by 5.62 units. The estimated co-efficients of X_1,X_3 and X_5 variable shows positive relationship with the criterion score individually. An increase in one unit of each and above 3 variables X_1, X_3 and X_5 will increase the criterion score by 0.650, 0.499 and 3.620 units respectively. This positive relationship is significant at 5 percent probability level on criterion score. The value of intercept term is 602.657.

The collective effect of all explanatory variables on explained variable is 3.426. The adjusted multiple correlation coefficient R^2 is 3.445. To test the significance of the collective effect of all independent variables on Y, F-test statistic has been computed. The estimated value of F is 174.42. It is significant at 5 percent probability level. D-statistic value is 1.176, expresses that there is no serial-correlation in the data.

Dropping of Long-Jump (X_4) variable from the model shows some decrease in the collective effect of the independent variables. It is observed as 17.2 percent. Hence, one can say that the dropping of X_4 variable will decrease the variables relation with the criterion score.

Comparing the estimated regression co-efficients between the models one and three, it is observed that there is no changes in the effects of variables 400 Mts. (X_2) and High Jump (X_3) on the score of Y. But it is observed that there is some decrease in the effect of High Jump (X_3), i.e., 1.4 percent. This decrease is a negligible effect on Y.

Observing the net effect of the variable 100 Mts. (X_1) there is a good increase i.e., 47.6 percent and Shot put i.e., 103 percent.

Dropping of Long Jump variable resulted

48 percent increase in weightage for 100 Mts.

2 percent increase in weightage for 400 Mts.

1.4 percent decrease in weightage for High Jump and

103 percent increase in weightage for Shot put scores.

The total variation in criterion score was decreased by 5 percent by dropping of Long Jump variable from the first model.

CONSTRUCTION OF NEW NORMS FOR PHYSICAL EFFICIENCY TEST

The purpose of the present study is to construct standards norms for Physical Efficiency Test for Physical Education Common Entrance Test. of Andhra Pradesh. Norms were constructed by using 'Hull-Scale', the scale that based on properties of normal curve. Hull Scale extends three and half standard deviations on either side of the mean. Investigator feels that this scale is more appropriate because the scores within the scale are well spread (than the T-scale) and the occurrence of extreme score falling outside 7 sigma limits is remote. At present a conversion table which is supplied by Government of Andhra Pradesh is used to allot the scores for various items (variables) i.e., 100 Mts., 800 Mts., (400 Mts. women), High Jump, Long Jump and Shot Put. These conversion tables fixes the score points for physical efficiency test items. Basically how these scores are allotted has no theoretical basis and if we want to revise the score how to obtain these scores is not clearly mentioned. To fill this gap, the present study helps to use and can be revised time to time to suite the needs of the Physical Education Common Entrance Test. This new method is developed to construct the norms which has a theoretical basis and authenticity.

Based on a statistical technique the following means and standard deviations of various items (variables) for men are obtained and given in the Table 4.7.

TABLE 4.7

MEANS AND STANDARD DEVIATIONS OF MEN TEST VARIABLES

	100 Mts.	*800 Mts.*	*High Jump*	*Long Jump*	*Shot Put*
MEAN	13.869	2.522	1.230	4.206	7.744
SD	1.239	0.36	0.29	0.643	2.012

The means and standard deviations of various items (Variables) for women are obtained and given in the following Table. 4.8

TABLE 4.8

MEANS AND STANDARD DEVIATIONS OF WOMEN TEST VARIABLES

	100 Mts.	*400 Mts.*	*High Jump*	*Long Jump*	*Shot Put*
MEAN	18.204	1.445	1.048	2.969	5.372
SD	2.678	0.215	0.149	0.539	1.132

The norms for men in 100 Mts., 800 Mts., High Jump, Long Jump and Shot Put were presented in the following Tables 4.9 - 4.13

The norms for women i.e., 100Mts. Run, 400Mts. Run, High Jump, Long Jump and Shotput are presented in the Tables 4.14 - 4.18.

FINDINGS OF THE PHYSICAL EFFICIENCY TEST NORMS (MEN AND WOMEN)

Critically comparing the new norms with the conversion norms (presently used) of various test items (variables) the following findings are drawn.

1) New norms given in Tables : 4.9 - 4.13 starts from 10-90 with an incremental value one, whereas conversion norms cover score points from 10-100 only.

2) The men test variable performance records compared as follows:

MEN TEST

VARIABLES	NEW NORMS		PRESENT NORMS	
	U.L	L.L.	U.L	L.L.
100 Mts. run	10.401sec.	- 17.337 sec.	12.0 sec.	- 17.4 sec
800 Mts. run	1.114sec.	- 4.330 sec.	2.00 sec.	- 2.59 sec
High Jump	2.042 Mts.	- 0.418 Mts.	5'6"	- 3'6"
Long Jump	6.006 Mts.	- 2.406 Mts.	21'6"	- 10'0"
Shot Put	13.680 Mts.	- 1.808Mts.	19.70 Mts.	- 1.50 Mts.

(U.L. = Upper Limits, L.L. = Lower Limits)

By comparing upper and lower limits for new norms with conversion norms one can conclude that new norms cause wider range than conversion norms in all items.

3) The women test variables performance records compared as follows

WOMEN TEST

VARIABLES	NEW NORMS		PRESENT NORMS	
	U.L	L.L.	U.L	L.L.
100 Mts. run	10.705 sec.	- 25.697 sec.	14.0 sec.	- 19.4 sec
400 Mts. run	0.443 sec.	- 2.450 sec.	1.04 sec.	- 1.56 sec
High Jump	1.465 Mts.	- 0.634 Mts.	4'6"	- 2'6"
Long Jump	4.478 Mts.	- 1.460 Mts.	18'6"	- 7'0"
Shot Put	8.542 Mts.	- 2.202 Mts.	19.70 Mts.	- 1.50 Mts.

(U.L. = Upper Limits, L.L. = Lower Limits)

By comparing upper and lower limits for new norms with conversion norms one can conclude that new norms cause wider range than conversion norms in all items.

4) New norms performance points measures more accurate i.e., measures upto 3 decimal points. Whereas conversion norms performance points are in single decimal point in 100 Mts., 800 Mts., and 400 Mts., and feet and inches in High Jump and Long Jump items.

5) Conversion norms score points are not continuously given and the incremental value is not uniform. Uniformity is most important criteria which is to be strictly maintained in any norms. This concept of uniformity is strictly maintained in the new norms.

6) Comparing various lower limits of the items, it is noticed in conversion norms that the score points are truncated at 10, which infact is not appropriate. Hence in the new norms it is extended to one i.e., in new norms the lower limits starts from10.

7) The range of the performance of items is increased in the new norms which helps in measuring the increasing as well as decreasing performance levels of the individuals, which ensures that for every individual participating in various items can fix a score points which is not possible in conversion norms.

8) In new norms the performance records of High Jump and Long Jump are measured in meters and centimeters, which is the latest method of measuring the performances, whereas in conversion norms measures in feet and inches.

9) Since the new norms are based on normal distribution, and are obtained through a specific procedure one can get the scores for any point of performance by using the Hull Scale, whereas it is not possible in the conversion norms.

Finally, it is estimated that new norms are more accurate, more utility and applicability in measuring the performances of the individuals.

TABLE—4.9

PHYSICAL EFFICIENCY TEST NORMS FOR WOMEN

NORMS FOR MEN IN 100 METERS RUN

Performance Seconds	*Score*	*Performance Seconds*	*Score*	*Performance Seconds*	*Score*	*Performance Seconds*	*Score*
10.401	90	12.135	70	13.869	50	15.603	30
10.488	89	12.221	69	13.955	49	15.689	29
10.574	88	12.308	68	14.042	48	15.776	28
10.661	87	12.395	67	14.129	47	15.863	27
10.748	86	12.481	66	14.215	46	15.949	26
10.835	85	12.568	65	14.302	45	16.037	25
10.921	84	12.655	64	14.389	44	16.123	24
11.008	83	12.741	63	14.475	43	16.210	23
11.095	82	12.828	62	14.562	42	16.297	22
11.181	81	12.915	61	14.649	41	16.383	21
11.268	80	13.002	60	14.736	40	16.470	20
11.355	79	13.088	59	14.822	39	16.557	19
11.441	78	13.175	58	14.909	38	16.643	18
11.528	77	13.262	57	14.996	37	16.730	17
11.615	76	13.348	56	15.082	36	16.817	16
11.701	75	13.435	55	15.169	35	16.904	15
11.788	74	13.522	54	15.256	34	16.990	14
11.874	73	13.608	53	15.342	33	17.077	13
11.961	72	13.695	52	15.429	32	17.164	12
12.048	71	13.782	51	15.516	31	17.250	11
						17.337	10

TABLE—4.10

NORMS FOR MEN IN 800 METERS RUN

Performance Min. Sec.	*Score*	*Performance Min. Sec.*	*Score*	*Performance Min. Sec.*	*Score*	*Performance Min. Sec.*	*Score*
1.114	90	2.020	70	2.522	50	3.426	30
1.140	89	2.043	69	2.542	49	3.451	29
1.164	88	2.068	68	2.572	48	3.476	28
1.189	87	2.093	67	2.597	47	3.501	27
1.214	86	2.118	66	3.022	46	3.520	26
1.240	85	2.144	65	3.048	45	3.552	25
1.265	84	2.169	64	3.077	44	3.577	24
1.290	83	2.194	63	3.098	43	4.002	23
1.315	82	2.219	62	3.123	42	4.207	22
1.340	81	2.224	61	3.148	41	4.052	21
1.366	80	2.270	60	3.174	40	4.078	20
1.391	79	2.295	59	3.199	39	4.103	19
1.416	78	2.320	58	3.224	38	4.128	18
1.441	77	2.345	57	3.249	37	4.153	17
1.467	76	2.370	56	3.274	36	4.178	16
1.492	75	2.396	55	3.300	35	4.204	15
1.517	74	2.421	54	3.325	34	4.229	14
1.520	73	2.440	53	3.330	33	4.254	13
1.568	72	2.471	52	3.370	32	4.279	12
1.592	71	2.496	51	3.401	31	4.304	11
						4.330	10

TABLE—4.11

NORMS FOR MEN IN HIGH-JUMP

Performance Mts. cm.	*Score*	*Performance Mts. cm.*	*Score*	*Performance Mts. cm.*	*Score*	*Performance Mts. cm.*	*Score*
2.042	90	1.636	70	1.230	50	0.824	30
2.022	89	1.616	69	1.210	49	0.804	29
2.001	88	1.595	68	1.189	48	0.783	28
1.981	87	1.575	67	1.169	47	0.763	27
1.961	86	1.555	66	1.149	46	0.743	26
1.941	85	1.535	65	1.129	45	0.723	25
1.920	84	1.514	64	1.108	44	0.702	24
1.900	83	1.494	63	1.088	43	0.682	23
1.880	82	1.474	62	1.068	42	0.662	22
1.859	81	1.453	61	1.047	41	0.641	21
1.839	80	1.433	60	1.027	40	0.621	20
1.819	79	1.413	59	1.007	39	0.601	19
1.798	78	1.392	58	0.986	38	0.580	18
1.778	77	1.372	57	0.966	37	0.560	17
1.758	76	1.352	56	0.946	36	0.540	16
1.738	75	1.332	55	0.926	35	0.520	15
1.717	74	1.311	54	0.905	34	0.499	14
1.697	73	1.291	53	0.885	33	0.479	13
1.677	72	1.271	52	0.865	32	0.459	12
1.656	71	1.250	51	0.844	31	0.438	11
						0.418	10

TABLE—4.12

NORMS FOR MEN IN LONG-JUMP

Performance Mts. cm.	*Score*	*Performance Mts. cm.*	*Score*	*Performance Mts. cm.*	*Score*	*Performance Mts. cm.*	*Score*
6.006	90	5.106	70	4.206	50	3.261	29
5.961	89	5.061	69	4.161	49	3.216	28
5.916	88	5.016	68	4.116	48	3.171	27
5.871	87	4.971	67	4.071	47	3.126	26
5.826	86	4.926	66	4.026	46	3.081	25
5.781	85	4.881	65	3.981	45	3.036	24
5.736	84	4.836	64	3.936	44	2.991	23
5.691	83	4.791	63	3.891	43	2.946	22
5.646	82	4.746	62	3.846	42	2.901	21
5.601	81	4.701	61	3.801	41	2.856	20
5.556	80	4.656	60	3.756	40	2.811	19
5.511	79	4.611	59	3.711	39	2.766	18
5.466	78	4.566	58	3.666	38	2.721	17
5.421	77	4.521	57	3.621	37	2.676	16
5.376	76	4.476	56	3.576	36	2.631	15
5.331	75	4.431	55	3.531	35	2.586	14
5.286	74	4.386	54	3.486	34	2.541	13
5.241	73	4.341	53	3.441	33	2.496	12
5.196	72	4.296	52	3.396	32	2.451	11
5.151	71	4.251	51	3.351	31	2.406	10
				3.306	30		

TABLE—4.13

NORMS FOR MEN IN SHOT-PUT (12 LBS)

Performance Mts. cm.	*Score*	*Performance Mts. cm.*	*Score*	*Performance Mts. cm.*	*Score*	*Performance Mts. cm.*	*Score*
13.680	90	10.712	70	7.744	50	4.776	30
13.532	89	10.564	69	7.596	49	4.628	29
13.383	88	10.415	68	7.447	48	4.479	28
13.235	87	10.267	67	7.299	47	4.331	27
13.086	86	10.118	66	7.150	46	4.182	26
12.938	85	9.970	65	7.002	45	4.034	25
12.790	84	9.822	64	6.854	44	3.886	24
12.641	83	9.673	63	6.705	43	3.737	23
12.493	82	9.525	62	6.557	42	3.589	22
12.344	81	9.376	61	6.408	41	3.440	21
12.196	80	9.228	60	6.260	40	3.292	20
12.048	79	9.080	59	6.112	39	3.144	19
11.899	78	8.931	58	5.963	38	2.995	18
11.751	77	8.783	57	5.815	37	2.847	17
11.602	76	8.634	56	5.666	36	2.698	16
11.454	75	8.486	55	5.518	35	2.550	15
11.306	74	8.338	54	5.370	34	2.402	14
11.157	73	8.189	53	5.221	33	2.253	13
11.009	72	8.041	52	5.073	32	2.105	12
10.860	71	7.892	51	4.924	31	1.956	11
						1.808	10

TABLE—4.14

NORMS FOR WOMEN IN 100 METERS RUN

Performance Seconds	*Score*	*Performance* Seconds	*Score*	*Performance* Seconds	*Score*	*Performance* Seconds	*Score*
10.705	90	14.453	70	18.201	50	21.949	30
10.892	89	14.640	69	18.388	49	22.136	29
11.080	88	14.828	68	18.576	48	22.324	28
11.267	87	15.015	67	18.763	47	22.511	27
11.455	86	15.203	66	18.951	46	22.699	26
11.642	85	15.390	65	19.138	45	22.886	25
11.829	84	15.577	64	19.325	44	23.073	24
12.017	83	15.765	63	19.513	43	23.261	23
12.204	82	15.952	62	19.700	42	23.448	22
12.392	81	16.140	61	19.888	41	23.636	21
12.579	80	16.327	60	20.075	40	23.823	20
12.766	79	16.514	59	20.262	39	24.010	19
12.954	78	16.702	58	20.450	38	24.198	18
13.141	77	16.889	57	20.637	37	24.385	17
13.329	76	17.077	56	20.825	36	24.573	16
13.516	75	17.264	55	21.012	35	24.760	15
13.703	74	17.451	54	21.199	34	24.947	14
13.891	73	17.639	53	21.387	33	25.135	13
14.078	72	17.826	52	21.574	32	25.322	12
14.266	71	18.014	51	21.762	31	25.510	11
						25.697	10

TABLE—4.15

NORMS FOR WOMEN IN 400 METERS RUN

Performance Min. Sec.	*Score*	*Performance Min. Sec.*	*Score*	*Performance Min. Sec.*	*Score*	*Performance Min. Sec.*	*Score*
0.443	90	1.140	70	1.450	50	2.150	30
0.458	89	1.160	69	1.460	49	2.160	29
0.473	88	1.170	68	1.480	48	2.180	28
0.488	87	1.190	67	1.490	47	2.190	27
0.503	86	1.200	66	1.510	46	2.210	26
0.518	85	1.220	65	1.520	45	2.220	25
0.533	84	1.230	64	1.540	44	2.240	24
0.548	83	1.250	63	1.550	43	2.250	23
0.563	82	1.260	62	1.570	42	2.270	22
0.578	81	1.228	61	1.580	41	2.280	21
0.594	80	1.290	60	2.000	40	2.300	20
1.010	79	1.310	59	2.010	39	2.310	19
1.024	78	1.320	58	2.030	38	2.330	18
1.042	77	1.340	57	2.040	37	2.340	17
1.054	76	1.350	56	2.060	36	2.360	16
1.070	75	1.370	55	2.070	35	2.370	15
1.080	74	1.380	54	2.090	34	2.390	14
1.100	73	1.400	53	2.100	33	2.400	13
1.110	72	1.410	52	2.120	32	2.420	12
1.130	71	1.420	51	2.130	31	2.430	11
						2.450	10

TABLE—4.16

NORMS FOR WOMEN IN HIGH-JUMP

Performance Mts. cm.	*Score*	*Performance Mts. cm.*	*Score*	*Performance Mts. cm.*	*Score*	*Performance Mts. cm.*	*Score*
1.465	90	1.258	70	1.050	50	0.842	30
1.455	89	1.247	69	1.039	49	0.831	29
1.445	88	1.237	68	1.029	48	0.821	28
1.434	87	1.226	67	1.018	47	0.810	27
1.424	86	1.216	66	1.008	46	0.800	26
1.414	85	1.206	65	0.998	45	0.790	25
1.403	84	1.195	64	0.987	44	0.779	24
1.393	83	1.185	63	0.977	43	0.769	23
1.382	82	1.174	62	0.966	42	0.758	22
1.372	81	1.164	61	0.956	41	0.748	21
1.362	80	1.154	60	0.946	40	0.737	20
1.351	79	1.143	59	0.935	39	0.727	19
1.341	78	1.133	58	0.925	38	0.717	18
1.330	77	1.122	57	0.914	37	0.706	17
1.320	76	1.112	56	0.904	36	0.696	16
1.310	75	1.102	55	0.894	35	0.686	15
1.299	74	1.091	54	0.883	34	0.675	14
1.289	73	1.081	53	0.873	33	0.665	13
1.278	72	1.070	52	0.862	32	0.654	12
1.268	71	1.060	51	0.852	31	0.644	11
						0.634	10

TABLE—4.17

NORMS FOR WOMEN IN LONG-JUMP

Performance Mts. cm.	*Score*	*Performance Mts. cm.*	*Score*	*Performance Mts. cm.*	*Score*	*Performance Mts. cm.*	*Score*
4.478	90	3.724	70	2.969	50	2.214	30
4.440	89	3.686	69	2.931	49	2.177	29
4.403	88	3.648	68	2.894	48	2.139	28
4.365	87	3.610	67	2.856	47	2.101	27
4.327	86	3.573	66	2.818	46	2.063	26
4.290	85	3.535	65	2.780	45	2.026	25
4.252	84	3.497	64	2.743	44	1.988	24
4.214	83	3.459	63	2.705	43	1.950	23
4.176	82	3.422	62	2.667	42	1.913	22
4.139	81	3.384	61	2.629	41	1.875	21
4.101	80	3.346	60	2.592	40	1.837	20
4.063	79	3.309	59	2.554	39	1.799	19
4.025	78	3.271	58	2.516	38	1.762	18
3.988	77	3.233	57	2.479	37	1.724	17
3.950	76	3.195	56	2.441	36	1.686	16
3.912	75	3.158	55	2.403	35	1.648	15
3.875	74	3.120	54	2.365	34	1.611	14
3.837	73	3.082	53	2.328	33	1.573	13
3.799	72	3.044	52	2.290	32	1.535	12
3.761	71	3.007	51	2.252	31	1.498	11
						1.460	10

TABLE—4.18

NORMS FOR WOMEN IN SHOT-PUT (8 LBS)

Performance Mts. cm.	*Score*	*Performance Mts. cm.*	*Score*	*Performance Mts. cm.*	*Score*	*Performance Mts. cm.*	*Score*
8.542	90	6.957	70	5.372	50	3.787	30
8.462	89	6.878	69	5.293	49	3.708	29
8.383	88	6.798	68	5.214	48	3.629	28
8.304	87	6.719	67	5.134	47	3.549	27
8.225	86	6.640	66	5.055	46	3.470	26
8.145	85	6.561	65	4.976	45	3.391	25
8.066	84	6.481	64	4.897	44	3.312	24
7.987	83	6.402	63	4.817	43	3.233	23
7.908	82	6.323	62	4.738	42	3.153	22
7.828	81	6.244	61	4.659	41	3.074	21
7.749	80	6.164	60	4.580	40	2.995	20
7.670	79	6.085	59	4.500	39	2.916	19
7.591	78	6.006	58	4.421	38	2.836	18
7.511	77	5.927	57	4.342	37	2.757	17
7.432	76	5.847	56	4.263	36	2.678	16
7.353	75	5.768	55	4.183	35	2.599	15
7.274	74	5.689	54	4.104	34	2.519	14
7.195	73	5.610	53	4.025	33	2.440	13
7.115	72	5.530	52	3.946	32	2.361	12
7.036	71	5.451	51	3.866	31	2.282	11
						2.202	10

CHAPTER—5

SUMMARY, CONCLUSIONS AND COMMENDATIONS

SUMMARY

Physical education emphasizes the importance of physical activities, as they are directly related to the growth and development of an individual. Physical fitness movement is another development that is received wide attention in all segments of the society.

Here the role of physical education teacher is vital, as he/ she has to attend various individuals with varying level of physical fitness and varying level of energy demands for carrying out their tasks. He should be trained well and should possess the knowledge regarding physical fitness.

The purpose of this study is construction of valid norms and standardizing the existing physical efficiency test items for physical education common entrance test in Andhra Pradesh. It helps to assess the students efficiency which will be the base for admission of the student into physical education courses in Andhra Pradesh.

For this study data have been collected from three regions of Andhra Pradesh i.e., Rayalaseema, Andhra and Telangana covering

23 districts consist of 1050 male and 628 female students in random sample represented the same numbers from each district. The age groups between 20 to 23 years were taken as subjects for the study. To standardise the data only those candidates who obtained the minimum standards (30 percent aggregate out of five items expected to qualify) are considered. Thus, the sample is filtered down to 851 male and 499 female candidates for the purpose of this study.

The aim of the study was to find out the association of independent variables i.e., 100 mts. run, 800 mts. run (400 mts. for women), High jump, Long jump and Shot-put, with criterion variable (some of the scores of five variables) to standardise and to select the valid test items for physical efficiency test in relation to physical education common entrance test in Andhra Pradesh. Further, the study extended to construct the new norms for the test items.

MEN–PHYSICAL EFFICIENCY TEST RESULTS

For this study statistical method "Multiple linear Regression Analysis" was applied to find out relationship of independent variables namely: 100 mts run (X_1), 800 mts run (X_2), High jump (X_3), Long jump (X_4) and shot put (X_5) with criterion score (Y) (some of the scores of five variables).

The estimated regression coefficient of all independent variables, except X_1 shows positive and significant effect on criterion score (Y). The coefficient of X_1 is negative and significant. It means an increase in one unit of X_1 variable will decrease the criterion score by 5.25 units. It represents the negative relationship with criterion score. The negative and significant value reveals that there is a scope to increase the standards and norms of Y by standardising the norms in X_1 variable. The estimated X_2, X_3, X_4, and X_5 variables show positive relationship with the criterion score individually. An increase in one unit of each and above four variable will increase the criterion score by 1.135, 1.411, 4.046 and 2.171 units respectively. This positive relationship is significant at 5 percent probability level on criterion score. The estimated values of R^2 is 2.064 and F–test is 327.80 and it is significant at 5 percent probability level.

From the correlation matrix it is observed that the High jump variable shows negative relationship with 800 mts. and positive relationship with 100 mts. and shot put variable. The High jump and Long jump variables having the positive correlation with each other. In the case of Long jump variable, positive relationship was observed with all explanatory variables. The relationship between shot-put and 800 mts. is negative whereas the other variables relationship with shot-put is positive. 100 mts. run having positive association with other variables independently. The 800 mts. run shows negative relationship with High jump variable.

In the second model, the functional relationship was established on explained variable (Y) dropping the High jump variable (X_3). The estimated regression coefficients of all independent variables except 100 Mts. run (X_1) shows positive and significant effect on criterion score (Y). The coefficient of X_1 is negative and significant. It represents the negative relationship with criterion score variable. It means an increase in one of unit in X_1 variable will decrease the criterion score by 4.84 units. An increase in one unit of X_2, X_4, and X_5 variables will increase the criterion score by 1.052, 4.521 and 2.508 units respectively. This positive relationship is significant at 5 percent probability level on Y. The multiple correlation coefficient R^2 is 1.822 and F- test is 468.89. The values are significant at 5 percent probability level.

By dropping of High jump variable (X_3), the collective effect of remaining variables on Y decreases 0.232 units. It shows that the net effect on High jump variable on Y is 0.232 units. Hence the effect of X_3 variable will decrease the 23 percent in total relationship with criterion score. Dropping of X_3 variable resulted 41 percent increase in weightage for 100 mts. score, 8 percent decrease in weightage for 800 mts. score, 47.5 percent increase in weightage for Long jump score and 33.7 percent increase in weightage for shot-put score. The total variation in criterion score was decreased by 23 percent was observed by dropping the High jump variable over the first model.

In the third model, Long jump variable (X_4) was dropped, then the functional relationship was established on explained variable Y. The estimated regression coefficient of all independent variables except X_1 shows positive and significant effect on criterion score Y. The coefficient of X_1 is negative and significant, it means an increase in one unit in X_1, variable will decrease the criterion score by 1.276, 1.992 and 3.335 units respectively. This positive relationship is significant at 5 percent probability level on criterion score. The estimated value of R^2 is 1.215 and F–test is 1197.51 and it is significant at 5 percent probability level. Comparing the first model, the dropping of X_4 variable from the test, it decreases 42 percent weightage on the criterion score Y.

The effect of dropping Long jump variable increases 200 percent in 100 mts. score 58 percent in High jump score and 126 percent in shot-put score and 14 percent in 800 mts. score. The total variation in criterion score was decreased by 41.1 percent by dropping of Long jump variable over first model.

WOMEN–PHYSICAL EFFICIENCY TEST RESULTS

The statistical technique which is applied for men, i.e., 'Multiple Linear Regression Analysis' was applied for women data. In the first model of the study, the estimated regression co-efficients of all independent variables except X_2 (400 Mts.) shows positive and significant effect on criterion score (Y). The co-efficient of X_2 is negative and significant. It means an increase in one unit of X_2 will decrease the criterion score by 5.64 units. It represents the negative relationship with criterion score. It reveals that there is a scope to increase the test value by standardising the norms of X_2 variable. The estimated X_1, X_3, X_4 and X_5 variables shows positive relationship with criterion score individually. This positive relationship with Y value is significant in the cases of X_3, X_4, X_5 variables only. In the case of X_1 variable, the relationship with Y is not significant. An increase in one unit of each and above four variables X_1, X_3, X_4 and X_5 will increase the criterion score by 0.174, 0.508, 1.756 and 2.587 units respectively.

The multiple correlation co-efficient R^2 value is 3.598, and the estimated F-test value is 136.55. It is inferred that the values are significant at 5 percent probability level.

The estimated correlation matrix shows that the 400 Mts. variable having negative relationship with the 100 Mts., and High jump. It shows positive relationship with Long Jump and Shot Put. The High Jump and Long Jump variables having positive correlation with each other. Long Jump is having positive relationship with all other variables. The relationship between Shot Put and other variables is positive. 100 Mts., having positive association with High Jump, Long Jump and Shot Put and negative relationship with 400 Mts. run. The 400 Mts. run shows negative relationship with High Jump and positive relationship with Long Jump and Shot Put variables.

In the second model High Jump X_3 variable was dropped. The relationship was established between criterion score (Y) and the independent variable X_1, X_2, X_4 and X_5. The estimated co-efficient of all independent variables except X2 shows the positive and significant effect on the Y. This positive relationship is significant at 5 percent probability level. In the case of X_1, it is observed that there is a positive and significant relationship at 10 percent probability level. The estimated R^2 is 3.555 and F-test value is 171.84. The values are significant at 5 percent probability level. Exclusion of High Jump variable, the values is estimated and it shows a decrease of 4.3 percent on criterion score over the first model. Dropping of High Jump variable the correlation matrix resulted as 14 percent increase in weightage for 100 Mts. score, 10 percent decrease in weightage for 400 Mts. score, 1 percent increase in weightage for Long Jump score and 8 percent increase in weightage for Shot Put score.

In the third model, by dropping the Long Jump variable (X_4) from the first model the functional relationship was estimated between the criterion score Y and the independent variables X_1, X_2, X_3, X_5. The regression coefficient of all independent variable except X_2 (400 Mts.) shows positive and significant effect on criterion score. An increase in one unit of X_2 variable will decrease the criterion score by 5.62 units, and other three variables X_1, X_3 and X_5 will increase the criterion score by 0.650, 0.494 and 3.620 units respectively. This positive relationship is significant at 5 percent probability level.

The estimated values of R^2 is 3.426 and F-test is 174.42 and it is significant at 5 percent probability level.

Dropping of Long Jump (X_4) variable from the model shows some decrease in the collective effect of the independent variables. It is observed as 17.2 percent. It shows that dropping of X_4 variable will decrease the variable relation with the criterion score.

The results of the correlation matrix after dropping Long Jump variable resulted as 48 percent increase in weightage for 100 Mts. 2 percent increase in weightage for 400 Mts. 1.4 percent decrease in weightage for High Jump score and 103 percent increase in weightage for Shot Put scores. The total variation in criterion score was decreased by 5 percent while dropping of Long Jump variable from the first model.

RESULTS OF PHYSICAL EFFICIENCY TEST NORMS FOR MEN AND WOMEN

Norms were constructed by using Hull scale. The scale that based on the properties of normal curve. Hull Scale extends 3.5 standard deviations on either side of the mean. Investigator feels that this scale is more appropriate because the scores within the scale are well spread.

Critically comparing the new norms with the conversion norms, it is noticed that the new norms are having better results than the conversion norms. Norms given in the present study the scores are covers from 1-100, whereas they are from 10-100 in conversion norms. The performance of men and women items finds lot of difference in upper and lower limits of the scores and performances in new norms whereas comparing with conversion norms. Conversion norm score points are not continuously given and the incremental value is not uniform whereas uniformity is strictly maintained in the new norms. It is find that the range of performance increase in new norms which helps in measuring the increasing as well as decreasing performance levels of the individuals. The performance records of High Jump and Long Jump are measured in meters and centimetres, which is more suitable method in present days whereas in present norms it measures in feet and inches. The lower limit scores are calculated from one in new norms whereas it is truncated at 10 in conversion study which infact is not appropriate in measuring the performance of individuals.

Finally, it is noticed that Hull scale is more appropriate and also has a theoretical background , which helps in construction of norms, for various items.

CONCLUSIONS

The analysis and conclusions of the present study was given in this chapter. The analysis was drawn individually both for men and women. From the analysis the following conclusions were drawn.

Physical Efficiency Test For Men

The estimated regression coefficient of all selected variables on criterion score, shows significant effect. The variable 100 Mts. run shows negative effect on criterion score. The negative and significant effect of this variable expresses there is some scope to increase the standards and norms of criterion score by standardising the norms of this variable 100mts. run. The remaining 4 variables having positive and significant relation with criterion score. It is observed that the effect of these variables is positive i.e., increasing the norms of these variables will increase the standards of the criterion score. From the value of multiple correlation coefficient, it can be inferred that the total effect of all variables is significant on criterion score. It means the norms of these independent variables have strengthen the standards of criterion score at significant level.

The estimated equation, after dropping High jump variable, will show the similar effect as compared to the first equation, when all variables are included in the model. Comparing the values of the multiple correlation coefficient of two models, 23 percent collective effect was decreased on criterion score by dropping the High jump variable. From the results of third model, when dropping the Long jump variable, the collective effect of variable on criterion score was decreased nearly 42 percent over the first model. Comparing these decreases (High jump 23 percent, Long jump 42 percent) in norms and standards of criterion score dropping the High jump variable than the Long jump variable is a good decision in standardising the test items and to construct norms for the test.

Physical Efficiency Test For Women

The estimated regression coefficient of all selected variables on criterion score shows significant effect. The X_2 (400 Mts.) variable shows negative effect on criterion score. The negative and significant effect of these variables expresses that there is some scope to increase the standards and norms of criterion score by standardising the norms of these 400mts. run. The remaining four variables having positive and significant relation with criterion score. It is observed that the effect of these variables is positive and by increasing the norms of these variables will strengthen the dependent variable in the test. From the values of multiple correlation coefficient, it can be inferred that the total effect of all variables is significant on criterion score. It means the norms of these independent variables are strengthening the standards of criterion score at significant level.

The estimated equations, after dropping High Jump variable, will show the similar effect as compared to the first model, when all variables are included in the model.

Comparing the values of the multiple correlation coefficients of two models, 4.3 percent collective effect was decreased on criterion score by dropping the High Jump variable. From the results of the third model, when dropping the Long Jump variable the collective effect of variable on criterion score was decreased nearly 17.3 percent over the first model.

Comparing these decreases (High Jump 4.2 percent, Long Jump 17.3 percent) in norms and standards of criterion score, dropping the High Jump variable than the Long Jump is a good decision in standardizing the test items and construction of norms for the test.

Norms for Physical Efficiency Test (Men and Women)

New norms are constructed by using 'Hull Scale' statistical technique. This method is having more authentic and appropriate to construct the norms. From the study the following conclusions are drawn.

- The norms for variables (Items) start from 10.90, with an incremental value one.
- The performance limits in either side (upper and lower) shows a lot of difference in both men and women tests.
- It measures in more accurate upto three decimal points.
- Uniformity is maintained in measuring performance i.e, incremental values are strictly maintained.

- The performance records of High Jump and Long Jump is measured in meters and inches, which is a latest method of measuring in the performance levels.
- The range in performance is increased, it helps in measuring the increasing as well as decreasing performances of the individual.
- Norms are constructed by using Hull Scale technique. It is more authentic and has more theoretical support.

RECOMMENDATIONS

Based on the conclusions of the study the following recommendations have been made :

1. For standardised physical efficiency test in Physical Education Common Entrance Test (PECET) four variables (items)test is suitable rather than five variables.
2. The study recommends that the standardised physical efficiency test for men is
    - 100 Mts. run to measure speed
    - 800 Mts. run to measure endurance
    - Long Jump to measure Leg explosive strength
    - Shot Put to measure arm and shoulder griddle strength
3. The study recommends the standardised physical efficiency test for women is
    - 100 Mts. run to measure speed
    - 400 Mts. run to measure endurance
    - Long Jump to measure leg explosive strength
    - Shot Put to measure arm and shoulder griddle strength
4. Study recommends that the elimination of High Jump item from the test will not effect much on test score.
5. Standardized norms for physical efficiency test were constructed for men and women tests.

6. Similar study may be conducted for further simplifying the test items.
7. Similar study may be recommended to standardise for various efficiency tests.
8. Present study gives an idea to formulate exact test to find out related components.
9. Present study gives guidelines to formulate standards and norms for test.
10. Present study helps to select standardised technique to measure and to fix correct norms for various physical efficiency tests, which are existing or coming up in future.

BIBLIOGRAPHY

1. AAHPERD Health Related Physical Fitness Technical Manual (Reston Va; American Alliance for Health, Physical, Education, Recreation and Dance, 1984).

2. AAHPHERD Health related physical fitness test manual Reston (Va. American alliance for health, Physical Education, Recreation and Dance, 1980).

3. Agnes R. Wayman "What to Measure in Physical Education", Research Quarterly, 1 (1930).

4. Agnes R. Wayman, "Testing and Scoring the Physical Efficiency of College Women", Research Quarterly, 1 (1930).

5. Agnes Wayman, "What to measure in Physical Education", Research Quarterly, Vol.1, No.2, 1930.

6. Allen Carpentar "Factors in Motor Educability" Research quarterly, Vol.-14 (No.4-1943).

7. Andrew S.Jackson, "Factor Analysis of Selected Muscular Strength and Motor performance tests". Research Quarterly, Vol.42, No.2, 1971.

8. Arnett Chappelle, "The Purdue Motor Fitness Test Batteries for Senior High School Girls". Research Quarterly, Vol.33, No.3, October 1962.

9. Arthur H. Steinhaus, "The Challenge of Health Education to the YMCA" cited by Wynn F. Updyke and Perry B. Johnson, Principles of Modern Physical Education, Health and Recreation (New York: Holt, Rinehart and Winston Inc., 1970).

10. Arthur J.Wendler, "A Critical analysis of test element used in Physical Education", Research Quarterly, Vol.9, No: 1938.

11. Athicha Pillai, "Computation of norms for 12-minutes run and walk among school boys", unpublished Doctoral thesis, Alagappa University, karaikudi, 1991.

12. Author's Guide AAHPERD Health-related Physical Fitness Manual as cited by Ted A.Baumgartner and Andrew S.Jackson Measurement for Evaluation in Physical Education and Exercise Science (3rd ed.) (Dubuque, IOWA: W.M.S. Brown Publishers, 1987).

13. Barrow Harold M., Mc Gee Rose Mary, "A Practical approach to measurement in Physical Education", 3rd Ed. (Philadelphia: Lea & Febiger, 1979).

14. Blair Steven N., Harold B. Falls and Russel R.Pate " A New Fitness Test", The Physician and Sports Medicine, 11:4 (April 1983), "A New Physical Fitness Test", The Physician and Sports Medicine.

15. C.H.Mecloy, "A Factor Analysis of Test of Endurance", Research Quarterly, Vol.27, No.1, 1956.

16. Cureton T.K., "Physical Fitness Appraisal and Guidance", (St. Lous: The C.V. Mosby Co., 1947).

17. D.Allen Philips and James E. Hornak. " Measurement and Evaluation in Physical Education", ed. John Willey and sons, Inc., New York, 1976.

18. Dale Mood, "Test of Physical Fitness Knowledge Construction Administration and Norms:" Research Quarterly, 42:1 (1971).

19. David R. Hopkins, "Factor Analysis of selected Basket Ball Skill Test", Research Quarterly,Vol.48, No.3, 1977.

20. Ebel., "Measuring Educational Achievement" as mentioned by Clarke & Clarke in Application of Measurement to Physical Education (New Jersey: Prentice Hall, 1987).

21. Edwin A. Fleishman, "The Dimensions of Physical Fitness-the Nationwide Normative and Developmental study of Basic Tests", Research Quarterly, 34:2 (May 1963).

22. Elizabeth G.Glover, "Physical Fitness test items in the first, second and Third grades". Masters thesis, Women College, University of North Carolina, 1962.

23. Elizabeth Powel and Eugene C. Home, "Motor ability tests for High School Girls", Research Quarterly, Vol.10, No.4, (1939).

24. Emerson R.W. "The American Schools, ed. American Literature of the Nineteenth Century" An Anthology: Eurasia Publishing House (Pvt.) Ltd., New Delhi (1955).

25. Frederick W.Cozen: "Strength tests and measures of general Athletic ability in college men", Research Quarterly, Vol.11, No.1, 1940.

26. Gladys Scott. M., "Physical efficiency test for College Women", Research Quarterly, Vol.19, No.1, 1948.

27. H. Harrison Clarke, "Definition of Physical Fitness" Journal of Physical Education and Recreation, 50, No.8 (Oct. 1979).

28. Harold B.Falls, "AAHPERD Implements New Health/Fitness Test", Physician and Sports Medicine, 8:6 (June 1979).

29. Harold M. Barrow and Rose Mary Mc Gee, "A Practical Approach to Measurement in Physical Education", (2nd Ed.) (Philadelphia: Lea & Febiger, 1979).

30. Harold M. Barrow, "Test of Motor Ability for College Men", Research Quarterly, 25:3 (October, 1954).

31. Harold M. Barrow, Rose Mary Mc Gee. "A Practical Approach to Measurement in Physical Education", 3rd Ed. (Philadelphia: Lea & Febigal, 1979).

32. Harold M. Barrow., Rose Mary Mc Gee., "A Practical Approach to Measurement in Physical Education", 3rd Ed. (Philadelphia: Leas & Febiger, 1979).

33. Harrison Clarke, "Application of Measurement to Health and Physical Education", (5th Ed.)(Englewood Cliffs, New Jercy: Prentice Hall Inc. 1976) p.30.

34. Henry J.Monotoye and Donald E. Lamphiear, "Grip and Arm Strength in Males and Females, Age 10 to 69", Research Quarterly, 48:1 (March 1977).

35. Hockey, Physical Fitness: A Pathway to Healthful Living. A.P. Publication (1989).

36. Lawrence A.Holding and Andrew S.Jackson, "New National Norms 'Y' Way to Physical Fitness", Journal of Physical Education, 78:4 (November/December1980), 44-45.

37. Lawry B.Fletcher, "The Relationship of Selected Factors to the Physical Fitness of Senior High School Boys in Arkanasa", Journal of Physical Education, (1968), 88.

38. Lueien Brouha and M.V. Ball, Canadian Red Cross Society's Meal Study, (Toronto; University of Toronto Press, 1952).

39. M.D. Hunter, "A Dictionary for Physical Education", (Bhoomington: Indian University Press, 1966).

40. Margaret J. Safrit, "Evaluation in Physical Education Assessing Motor Behaviour", (Englewood Cliffs, New Jersey: Prentice Hall Inc., 1981).

41. Marvin A. Zuidema and Ted A.Baumgartner, "Second Factor Analysis study of Physical fitness tests", Research Quarterly, Vol.45, No.3, 1974.

42. Mary Evangeline or Cornor, Thomas Kirk Wraton, "Motor Fitness tests for high school girls", Research Quarterly, Vol.16, (M, 1945).

43. N.E. Gronlund, Measurement and Evaluation in Teaching (4th ed.) cited by Larry O.Hensley, "Current Measurement and Evaluation Practices in Professional PE", Journal sof Physical Education, Recreation and Dance, 61, 3 (1990).

44. Paul A. Hunsicker and Guy G.Reiff, AAHPERD Youth Fitness Test Manual; Rev.ed. (Reston.Va: American alliance for Health and Physical Education, Recreation and Dance, 1976).

45. Paul Bewbold, "Statistics for Business and Economics", Prentice Hall International, 2nd ed., 1988.

46. Robson, "A simple Physical Fitness Test Battery for Elementary School Children", SNIPES Journal, I:2, (April -1978).

47. S. C. Gupta and V. K. Kapoor, "Fundamentals of Applied Statistics", Sultan Chand & Sons, 3rd ed., 1994.

48. Solomon Faine, Devis T.Mathews. "Physical Fitness tests on Newzealand School Children", Research Quarterly, Vol.22, (Dec. 1951),.

49. Ted A. Baugartner, Andrew S. Jackson., "Measurement for Evaluation in Physical Education and Exercise Science", 3rd Ed. (lowa: W.C. Brown Pub., 1982).

50. Texas Governor Commission on Physical Fitness - Motor Ability tests, Texas Youth Fitness Test, Austin, Texas, 1973.

51. The Andhra Pradesh Gazette (Published by authority, No.22, May 1989). Government of Andhra Pradesh.

52. The Andhra Pradesh Gazette, (Published by the Authority No.22, Hyderabad, 1989).

53. Ted A. Baugartner, Andrew S. Jackson., "Measurement for Evaluation in Physical Education and Exercise Science", 3rd Ed. (lowa: W.C. Brown Pub., 1982).

54. Victor C.Dunder, "A Multiple strength index of general motor ability", Research Quarterly, Vol.4, No.3, 1936.

55. W.L. Foster,: "A Test of Physical Efficiency", American Physical Education Review, 1941.

56. Wilma K.Miller, "Achievement Levels in Basket ball skills for Women Physical Education Major", Research Quarterly, 25:4, (December 1954).

APPENDIX-1

PECET-PHYSICAL EFFICIENCY TEST RAW SCORES (MEN)

S.No.	100M	800M	High	Long	Shot
1	12.09	2.34	4.70	14.11	8.11
2	14.10	2.56	4.50	13.01	8.64
3	14.05	2.49	3.11	13.03	7.65
4	15.00	3.00	4.50	12.07	7.88
5	13.54	3.07	3.90	14.04	6.22
6	13.08	3.04	3.70	12.11	7.09
7	15.00	3.00	4.01	12.10	7.07
8	13.00	2.49	4.70	14.02	8.35
9	13.03	2.29	4.70	14.11	8.75
10	14.01	2.57	4.30	14.02	8.55
11	12.10	2.33	4.70	15.02	8.90
12	14.09	2.53	4.50	12.03	8.61
13	14.08	3.17	3.90	11.10	6.05
14	14.03	2.49	4.00	12.10	6.09
15	13.05	2.49	4.50	15.05	9.09
16	13.06	3.00	4.11	13.05	8.65
17	13.07	2.47	4.90	15.05	9.02
18	15.03	3.29	3.90	11.05	8.15

Contd.

1	*2*	*3*	*4*	*5*	*6*
19	12.75	2.36	4.30	18.04	8.75
20	12.06	2.12	4.60	17.02	13.01
21	15.00	2.05	4.20	12.05	6.21
22	14.01	3.17	4.90	13.01	8.05
23	14.01	3.11	4.50	13.03	6.06
24	14.00	3.12	4.01	13.08	7.06
25	13.08	2.43	4.70	13.05	8.35
26	12.08	3.15	4.70	13.11	9.35
27	16.59	3.17	0.00	11.06	6.08
28	13.01	2.37	4.70	15.04	7.59
29	13.00	2.29	4.90	16.08	9.04
30	14.08	2.34	4.30	13.06	7.75
31	13.06	2.03	4.50	14.02	7.75
32	13.06	2.38	4.70	14.04	9.22
33	13.07	2.29	4.01	14.07	6.81
34	13.84	2.43	4.07	14.01	6.90
35	12.08	3.05	4.90	15.01	7.52
36	14.00	2.31	3.11	13.10	7.05
37	12.08	2.15	4.10	16.00	9.05
38	14.08	2.48	4.50	14.06	6.82
39	13.09	2.37	4.30	15.02	7.72
40	15.05	2.42	3.11	11.04	8.22
41	12.78	2.03	4.11	16.01	10.37
42	16.00	0.00	0.00	12.01	8.05
43	16.08	3.12	3.11	11.08	6.53
44	12.09	2.48	4.11	15.07	8.82
45	14.05	3.06	4.30	12.11	8.12
46	14.08	3.00	4.50	12.04	7.48
47	12.08	2.40	4.30	16.06	9.45
48	14.00	3.11	4.01	13.05	6.35
49	13.03	2.57	3.90	12.06	9.78
50	14.04	2.56	3.70	11.10	6.14

Contd.

1	*2*	*3*	*4*	*5*	*6*
51	14.03	3.08	3.11	13.06	7.94
52	14.05	2.42	3.11	13.00	6.65
53	13.01	2.41	4.50	14.05	8.74
54	15.04	2.34	3.90	11.08	5.62
55	14.02	2.55	4.70	14.01	5.87
56	14.01	2.50	4.30	13.03	7.24
57	15.08	2.59	3.11	11.04	6.53
58	14.05	2.39	0.00	12.11	6.06
59	14.04	2.32	4.30	13.02	7.32
60	14.02	2.56	3.90	12.02	5.66
61	13.03	2.43	4.01	14.02	8.54
62	14.06	3.12	4.30	13.05	7.98
63	13.78	2.35	4.01	13.05	6.60
64	12.06	2.52	4.90	16.02	8.62
65	14.08	3.22	3.90	10.04	6.49
66	14.08	3.32	4.30	13.00	7.20
67	13.09	3.06	4.10	13.04	8.56
68	13.01	3.04	4.50	14.06	8.04
69	13.06	2.33	4.70	16.00	8.34
70	14.37	3.00	4.90	13.02	9.10
71	13.04	2.53	4.10	15.11	7.18
72	13.05	2.39	4.70	16.01	6.76
73	14.03	2.59	3.90	13.04	8.04
74	15.02	3.44	3.90	13.05	8.86
75	15.00	3.15	3.90	14.02	6.10
76	14.75	3.44	3.11	12.07	6.80
77	14.02	3.00	4.30	12.02	7.94
78	15.05	3.01	4.10	11.08	7.00
79	14.02	3.03	3.11	12.05	7.31
80	13.06	2.56	4.70	15.01	7.12
81	20.08	0.00	3.90	3.06	6.23
82	14.00	3.07	4.30	15.00	5.74

Contd.

1	*2*	*3*	*4*	*5*	*6*
83	16.02	2.56	3.11	12.11	7.80
84	14.03	2.47	4.70	13.07	6.64
85	12.00	2.01	5.01	17.03	8.82
86	13.04	2.32	5.03	16.02	[illegible].90
87	14.07	3.00	4.05	14.07	7.83
88	16.00	3.06	3.90	13.05	6.40
89	14.19	2.47	4.05	13.08	9.05
90	14.01	2.36	4.60	14.07	9.08
91	13.04	2.42	4.01	13.07	8.54
92	15.03	3.05	4.01	12.01	7.54
93	13.00	2.28	5.03	15.09	7.94
94	12.09	3.17	4.90	16.06	9.30
95	14.03	3.28	3.11	14.00	9.58
96	14.06	0.00	3.11	12.06	6.36
97	13.07	2.41	4.01	13.01	9.46
98	14.03	2.52	4.11	13.10	8.10
99	14.08	2.53	3.70	12.11	7.38
100	13.08	2.20	4.11	16.11	9.42
101	14.28	2.52	4.50	13.02	6.86
102	13.06	3.05	4.50	14.03	7.88
103	13.09	2.32	4.30	14.05	7.01
104	12.05	2.16	4.90	17.00	7.82
105	15.08	2.45	4.01	13.00	7.44
106	14.01	2.43	4.90	14.08	7.68
107	14.05	2.33	4.90	13.02	8.17
108	14.05	2.27	4.01	14.00	6.09
109	15.01	3.07	3.90	11.11	7.35
110	13.06	2.41	4.50	14.06	7.12
111	13.05	2.29	3.70	14.04	6.94
112	13.04	2.27	4.30	13.07	8.08
113	15.00	3.02	4.30	12.03	6.08
114	13.06	2.37	4.01	14.06	6.22

Contd.

1	*2*	*3*	*4*	*5*	*6*
115	15.00	3.13	3.90	12.01	6.09
116	14.06	2.52	4.30	13.09	8.54
117	13.04	2.44	4.90	15.01	6.96
118	12.04	2.39	4.90	14.05	8.01
119	16.02	3.05	3.11	11.06	7.78
120	13.18	2.28	4.30	14.06	7.24
121	13.00	2.49	4.70	15.06	9.76
122	12.04	2.03	5.01	16.09	9.07
123	14.32	2.31	4.10	14.01	7.28
124	16.02	3.02	0.00	11.04	7.42
125	13.04	2.32	4.70	14.06	7.58
126	14.00	3.38	4.70	11.01	7.02
127	12.04	2.32	4.70	15.03	6.82
128	14.18	2.42	4.01	15.00	6.72
129	12.09	3.00	4.90	16.08	7.06
130	11.08	2.18	4.90	16.04	8.38
131	14.00	2.05	3.90	13.00	6.06
132	14.04	2.42	4.70	13.01	6.01
133	15.72	3.11	4.01	10.05	8.06
134	14.09	2.05	4.01	12.01	6.09
135	14.08	2.04	3.90	12.09	6.47
136	12.07	2.35	4.30	15.05	7.07
137	14.05	2.03	3.70	12.05	7.65
138	15.03	2.54	0.00	10.02	7.07
139	14.05	2.49	4.30	14.06	7.78
140	14.06	2.33	4.90	12.02	8.10
141	15.43	3.12	4.01	12.06	7.65
142	13.00	2.26	4.01	14.09	9.00
143	14.03	2.33	4.30	14.05	8.35
144	15.01	2.55	4.70	13.09	7.06
145	13.04	3.03	3.11	14.01	6.92
146	14.03	2.49	4.50	13.01	8.01

Contd.

1	*2*	*3*	*4*	*5*	*6*
147	14.03	3.14	4.01	11.00	6.06
148	15.02	3.07	3.70	13.02	6.56
149	13.04	2.43	4.01	13.07	8.01
150	14.00	2.44	3.70	13.05	4.08
151	13.00	2.29	4.70	16.07	5.66
152	14.03	3.03	5.30	14.05	6.95
153	16.00	2.53	3.70	12.06	6.65
154	12.09	2.34	4.30	15.08	8.60
155	13.00	2.03	4.90	16.08	7.63
156	12.06	2.37	4.70	16.08	7.07
157	14.02	2.38	3.70	13.07	6.08
158	13.01	2.48	4.30	13.08	6.08
159	15.03	2.40	4.01	12.05	6.10
160	14.03	2.46	4.50	13.05	7.00
161	15.08	2.40	3.90	12.00	6.10
162	14.05	2.31	4.50	15.07	7.40
163	14.04	2.47	4.70	14.04	7.85
164	13.08	2.25	4.30	15.00	6.75
165	13.05	2.27	4.50	15.05	8.66
166	15.04	2.55	4.01	14.08	7.30
167	14.00	3.07	4.30	14.04	8.43
168	14.01	2.47	4.01	13.06	7.90
169	14.00	3.47	3.90	14.00	8.30
170	15.01	3.04	3.70	12.00	6.45
171	13.09	2.45	4.01	13.00	6.56
172	12.09	2.36	4.01	14.11	6.00
173	14.00	3.02	4.01	12.10	9.82
174	15.04	3.24	4.50	13.06	5.50
175	13.05	2.40	4.50	12.06	7.55
176	15.00	2.41	3.90	11.05	7.08
177	13.00	2.49	4.30	14.10	8.09
178	14.03	3.25	3.11	12.08	9.35

Contd.

1	*2*	*3*	*4*	*5*	*6*
179	12.09	2.28	4.90	14.06	6.07
180	16.09	0.00	0.00	0.00	6.16
181	16.07	3.24	4.50	9.01	6.33
182	13.02	2.35	4.50	13.01	8.25
183	12.01	2.29	4.90	15.11	7.66
184	13.05	2.31	4.70	14.06	6.17
185	12.07	2.34	4.01	15.05	6.70
186	12.00	2.45	4.90	16.04	9.05
187	14.08	3.00	3.60	13.06	6.07
188	14.01	2.48	4.01	14.10	8.20
189	14.08	3.06	3.11	10.08	9.10
190	14.04	2.35	4.01	13.10	7.85
191	14.03	2.04	3.70	10.07	6.90
192	14.05	2.59	4.01	13.07	7.05
193	12.05	2.38	4.90	15.10	7.90
194	12.08	2.28	4.90	15.06	8.72
195	14.08	3.06	4.30	12.00	8.18
196	14.01	3.17	4.70	13.09	9.56
197	12.08	2.35	4.70	16.03	8.40
198	13.05	2.34	4.01	15.06	8.79
199	12.05	2.22	4.50	17.00	7.17
200	13.28	3.14	4.50	14.00	12.27
201	12.08	2.55	4.70	14.00	6.43
202	13.01	2.54	4.01	13.03	7.27
203	12.03	2.39	3.11	16.08	10.42
204	12.04	2.38	4.70	15.10	7.12
205	17.01	3.53	3.60	9.10	5.49
206	15.00	2.54	4.30	12.00	8.00
207	14.00	2.41	4.30	15.10	9.10
208	12.05	2.38	3.60	14.09	8.60
209	12.07	2.33	4.90	17.00	10.57
210	12.08	2.31	3.01	17.06	8.37

Contd.

1	*2*	*3*	*4*	*5*	*6*
211	12.08	2.32	4.90	17.04	8.90
212	13.05	2.33	4.70	15.06	9.22
213	14.05	3.00	4.30	15.00	7.98
214	15.01	2.57	4.01	13.08	8.32
215	13.07	2.57	4.01	14.05	8.16
216	12.06	2.39	5.90	17.00	9.62
217	14.03	2.40	4.70	14.04	10.52
218	14.09	2.49	3.11	15.00	6.33
219	16.02	3.15	0.00	7.05	5.55
220	14.08	3.03	0.00	9.00	6.64
221	14.00	2.46	4.30	13.11	8.29
222	12.00	2.11	4.30	18.11	10.00
223	15.08	2.50	3.11	12.08	5.90
224	14.08	3.24	3.90	15.04	8.09
225	12.08	3.12	4.90	15.06	9.07
226	13.04	2.29	4.30	12.05	8.23
227	12.04	2.49	5.05	16.11	8.26
228	13.06	3.04	4.30	15.06	8.19
229	15.00	2.59	3.11	12.02	9.00
230	16.07	3.00	4.30	11.15	8.12
231	13.01	2.29	4.70	15.00	7.70
232	13.06	3.00	4.01	13.08	9.09
233	13.00	2.40	4.01	14.09	8.62
234	13.05	2.18	4.70	13.11	7.14
235	12.06	2.09	4.90	16.07	8.89
236	13.05	2.20	4.30	13.03	6.47
237	14.02	3.02	4.11	15.00	9.06
238	15.05	3.09	4.30	11.11	6.95
239	15.05	2.35	3.11	14.08	10.65
240	15.04	3.56	0.00	12.05	75.70
241	14.00	2.39	4.30	14.11	10.25
242	14.04	2.53	4.50	13.04	7.00

Contd.

1	2	3	4	5	6
243	13.05	2.43	4.30	15.00	7.40
244	13.02	2.34	4.50	16.00	8.07
245	14.00	2.33	4.30	14.07	7.13
246	14.08	2.53	5.01	14.04	8.50
247	15.05	3.06	3.90	13.03	6.15
248	14.09	3.25	4.50	14.01	8.00
249	14.04	2.47	4.50	13.11	8.83
250	14.05	3.08	3.90	12.09	7.68
251	14.02	2.56	3.90	13.06	9.68
252	13.04	2.50	4.70	16.02	10.85
253	12.09	2.44	4.70	13.11	7.85
254	12.09	2.48	4.70	16.08	11.15
255	13.05	2.29	4.70	14.06	8.95
256	13.07	2.33	5.30	16.01	9.45
257	12.08	2.11	5.01	14.08	10.10
258	13.01	3.02	4.50	10.11	8.75
259	12.03	2.23	5.01	17.06	8.08
260	14.97	3.21	3.11	12.09	9.09
261	14.05	2.57	4.30	10.11	6.01
262	13.41	2.56	4.30	14.06	6.85
263	14.05	2.51	3.90	11.11	6.03
264	12.04	2.36	4.90	15.01	7.08
265	14.04	3.00	4.30	12.04	8.75
266	15.07	3.25	3.90	11.04	8.06
267	14.02	2.58	3.11	13.01	7.05
268	14.05	3.00	4.50	13.07	7.06
269	13.00	2.38	4.50	14.08	7.06
270	12.78	2.36	5.01	16.08	7.04
271	14.08	3.00	3.11	11.02	8.01
272	13.00	2.45	4.01	14.04	7.35
273	13.01	3.01	4.30	13.04	8.55
274	13.01	2.46	4.90	14.02	10.95

Contd.

1	*2*	*3*	*4*	*5*	*6*
275	13.09	2.44	4.50	14.09	7.75
276	14.05	3.15	4.70	14.09	8.65
277	13.44	0.00	4.30	14.05	7.09
278	14.02	3.10	4.90	14.08	8.10
279	14.00	2.54	4.70	14.08	9.86
280	14.05	2.55	3.90	14.02	8.30
281	15.00	3.00	4.70	13.03	8.70
282	16.07	3.23	3.70	8.03	6.07
283	12.09	2.23	4.50	15.09	8.80
284	14.09	2.09	4.50	15.08	11.55
285	13.05	2.39	4.30	15.05	8.15
286	13.08	3.00	4.30	13.08	8.15
287	13.05	2.54	3.11	13.04	6.90
288	13.03	2.53	3.11	13.05	8.11
289	13.01	2.35	4.90	15.06	8.48
290	12.09	2.26	4.11	16.04	9.74
291	12.07	2.31	4.11	16.02	8.76
292	15.25	3.18	4.01	12.03	6.03
293	14.03	2.45	4.07	13.09	8.25
294	13.02	2.17	4.09	14.00	9.25
295	13.08	3.00	3.11	13.01	8.16
296	12.05	2.38	4.08	16.01	9.14
297	15.06	2.56	4.07	9.01	7.14
298	13.04	2.44	3.11	13.00	7.09
299	11.08	2.02	4.11	16.08	9.08
300	14.03	2.54	4.70	13.08	5.56
301	17.00	3.24	3.60	8.07	7.14
302	15.01	3.00	3.09	10.04	7.04
303	14.00	2.03	4.01	13.07	7.98
304	12.09	2.38	4.07	14.11	8.86
305	13.00	3.02	4.90	14.01	8.45
306	13.01	2.34	4.05	14.00	8.56

Contd.

1	*2*	*3*	*4*	*5*	*6*
307	13.04	2.24	4.10	13.03	8.96
308	14.00	3.09	4.30	12.00	8.06
309	15.03	3.21	3.70	9.06	7.15
310	14.05	2.03	4.80	13.00	8.08
311	12.08	2.05	4.01	14.09	8.08
312	16.09	3.14	4.30	15.09	9.08
313	14.00	3.08	3.90	12.02	5.09
314	11.08	2.41	4.11	17.07	10.30
315	14.09	3.38	3.06	12.04	6.85
316	15.00	3.07	3.10	12.03	8.50
317	14.05	3.00	3.10	12.00	7.20
318	15.39	3.09	3.10	13.02	6.00
319	14.25	3.25	3.06	14.07	9.65
320	15.00	3.15	3.08	12.02	6.35
321	14.06	3.04	4.02	14.00	7.95
322	12.93	2.27	4.10	18.00	10.00
323	13.00	2.47	4.10	14.07	7.35
324	15.03	3.25	4.00	13.02	7.05
325	13.01	2.47	4.06	13.08	7.90
326	14.06	2.39	4.00	12.00	5.10
327	15.06	3.26	3.10	13.00	6.10
328	15.06	2.47	3.10	14.02	6.72
329	14.00	3.09	4.04	14.00	7.75
330	14.56	3.17	4.06	14.00	7.70
331	15.43	2.54	4.00	13.00	6.80
332	13.86	2.48	4.00	13.00	7.30
333	14.02	2.59	4.00	13.04	6.55
334	18.05	0.00	0.00	10.10	5.80
335	14.00	3.02	4.06	13.04	8.55
336	11.08	2.24	4.04	19.00	6.60
337	16.49	2.59	0.00	11.09	5.82
338	15.60	3.16	4.04	12.06	6.80

Contd.

1	*2*	*3*	*4*	*5*	*6*
339	14.56	2.37	4 00	15.07	7.00
340	14.05	2.57	4.10	14.03	5.90
341	13.00	2.29	4.10	15.04	7.60
342	14.03	3.15	4.04	15.05	7.18
343	13.08	2.58	4.02	15.06	7.50
344	14.35	2.57	4.00	13.10	6.53
345	17.06	3.40	0.00	11.06	4.68
346	14.01	2.27	4.02	15.07	7.11
347	13.09	2.43	4.04	15.03	7.23
348	13.75	2.42	4.04	17.00	6.85
349	15.02	3.30	4.02	14.00	6.25
350	15.03	3.08	4.06	15.00	6.20
351	13.29	2.32	4.06	15.00	8.61
352	13.08	2.41	3.06	14.02	7.22
353	14.02	2.53	4.02	15.00	7.92
354	12.00	2.46	4.06	15.04	8.87
355	15.25	3.18	3.10	13.08	6.81
356	13.74	2.37	4.04	15.00	5.96
357	14.30	2.49	4.04	13.06	7.38
358	15.05	3.22	0.00	12.04	6.60
359	14.15	3.21	3.10	13.04	8.13
360	13.59	2.21	4.06	15.10	7.41
361	15.24	3.46	4.02	15.06	6.85
362	12.00	2.13	4.04	18.06	6.92
363	13.59	2.38	4.10	15.09	7.50
364	12.86	2.40	4.10	16.05	6.98
365	13.58	2.44	4.02	15.08	8.18
366	16.01	2.54	3.10	12.06	6.30
367	13.11	2.48	4.08	14.08	7.21
368	13.24	3.05	4.10	15.06	8.69
369	14.16	2.41	4.04	16.00	8.55
370	12.08	2.48	4.06	14.08	8.95

Contd.

1	*2*	*3*	*4*	*5*	*6*
371	13.96	2.51	4.00	13.03	7.70
372	15.71	3.05	3.06	14.00	8.53
373	12.36	2.39	4.06	16.10	9.30
374	13.02	2.41	4.02	13.02	8.55
375	16.77	3.27	3.06	11.06	6.85
376	13.46	2.48	4.10	14.07	8.67
377	13.43	2.39	3.10	14.03	7.83
378	12.00	2.36	4.04	14.02	6.25
379	13.77	2.42	4.06	17.00	7.85
380	14.17	2.59	4.02	14.06	9.07
381	13.24	2.46	4.02	14.01	8.20
382	13.51	2.26	4.04	15.00	6.97
383	17.80	3.31	3.06	13.00	6.63
384	15.04	3.17	3.10	12.10	6.75
385	15.24	3.45	4.00	11.05	6.50
386	13.06	3.03	5.00	16.00	8.25
387	14.43	2.52	3.10	14.03	6.78
388	13.91	3.39	4 04	14.04	8.63
389	14.04	3.20	3.10	14.04	9.71
390	13.56	2.42	4.02	15.01	8.28
391	13.42	2.50	4.04	17.02	7.80
392	13.08	2.35	4.04	15.07	8.25
393	13.32	3.13	4.10	12.09	9.48
394	14.06	2.57	4.08	15.00	8.25
395	14.08	2.53	4.04	13.01	6.35
396	14.88	2.51	4.00	14.06	7.55
397	14.05	3.13	4.06	13.08	9.69
398	17.05	3.34	3.06	8.08	6.51
399	13.44	3.27	5.00	17.03	8.25
400	14.99	2.53	4.00	15.02	7.25
401	14.06	2.59	4.00	14.08	7.20
402	13.05	2.52	4.02	16.08	7.10

Contd.

1	*2*	*3*	*4*	*5*	*6*
403	15.04	2.49	3.08	12.00	6.70
404	13.52	3.14	5.02	17.08	8.60
405	15.02	3.25	3.08	12.05	7.30
406	15.27	2.45	3.08	13.03	6.65
407	13.06	3.00	3.08	13.05	6.93
408	14.03	2.54	4.02	14.07	9.15
409	14.08	3.00	3.06	12.10	6.80
410	13.08	2.39	4.04	16.00	9.05
411	15.31	3.06	3.06	10.04	7.05
412	14.05	3.09	4.00	15.05	7.30
413	14.06	3.00	4.04	13.00	8.96
414	14.06	3.04	4.02	15.00	8.55
415	14.05	3.12	4.10	16.03	7.78
416	13.97	2.52	4.08	16.10	8.72
417	13.04	2.24	4.04	16.10	9.05
418	13.25	2.40	4.10	16.08	8.48
419	12.05	2.40	5.00	17.03	7.72
420	12.05	2 35	4.08	16.06	7.70
421	12.05	2.29	4.04	16.02	7.98
422	14.08	3.19	3.10	15.02	6.37
423	12.07	2.25	4.06	17.05	7.79
424	12.66	2.22	5.02	17.00	7.26
425	16.04	3.02	4.00	12.05	6.82
426	13.32	2.22	4.06	16.02	7.56
427	15.01	3.11	3.06	12.06	7.23
428	12.05	2.50	5.00	17.05	8.47
429	14.06	3.04	4.02	13.09	7.12
430	13.02	3.04	4.04	15.07	7.59
431	14.07	3.06	3.08	15.00	7.94
432	14.56	2.48	3.08	14.00	7.51
433	13.09	2.59	4.02	14.00	8.05
434	14.07	2.39	4.02	15.00	6.83

Contd.

1	2	3	4	5	6
435	13.02	3.00	4.04	16.05	8.28
436	14.05	2.33	4.00	14.00	8.52
437	15.02	3.10	3.08	13.05	6.90
438	13.45	2.59	4.02	14.03	6.60
439	12.13	3.06	4.06	14.08	8.40
440	14.02	2.37	4.04	13.10	7.20
441	13.88	2.48	4.06	15.10	6.90
442	13.00	2.41	4.04	17.00	8.08
443	13.06	3.00	4.10	14.07	10.20
444	13.47	2.41	3.08	14.07	8.60
445	14.07	3.03	4.04	14.05	8.95
446	13.08	2.40	4.06	16.02	8.75
447	13.02	2.50	4.04	15.01	7.67
448	14.70	2.50	4.00	14.00	6.11
449	15.00	2.55	4.10	16.08	7.30
450	15.42	2.44	0.00	13.05	5.60
451	15.16	3.16	3.10	11.06	6.50
452	14.19	2.49	4.06	12.05	8.30
453	20.04	0.00	3.06	10.04	5.85
454	13.07	3.02	4.06	15.00	6.10
455	15.00	3.19	4.06	11.00	6.05
456	14.07	3.06	4.00	13.00	7.15
457	14.13	2.46	4.04	15.02	6.90
458	13.01	2.43	4.08	16.08	7.20
459	13.40	2.30	4.02	14.10	7.00
460	12.00	3.05	4.04	16.10	9.00
461	15.17	3.26	4.00	14.03	8.40
462	13.87	2.21	4.00	14.07	7.50
463	15.07	3.03	4.02	11.02	6.60
464	13.37	2.50	4.10	15.02	7.45
465	12.83	2.46	4.08	15.02	8.50
466	14.23	2.40	4.10	15.02	9.10

Contd.

12	3	4	5	6	
467	13.04	2.40	4.08	16.06	7.45
468	14.15	2.39	4.04	14.05	6.85
469	14.07	3.54	4.00	14.06	7.75
470	12.07	2.51	5.00	16.11	8.15
471	15.00	2.50	4.04	14.01	8.25
472	15.78	2.59	4.00	11.03	6.65
473	14.63	3.12	4.08	15.01	7.85
474	15.64	3.36	3.08	12.08	6.75
475	12.75	2.22	4.06	15.04	6.05
476	14.99	2.55	3.10	13.04	7.20
477	15.05	2.56	4.02	13.11	7.80
478	14.79	3.18	3.10	13.06	7.12
479	13.01	2.28	3.10	13.07	7.60
480	13.77	2.52	4.02	14.00	7.25
481	12.34	2.30	5.02	17.03	10.25
482	14.02	3.09	4.02	12.08	7.40
483	14.35	3.23	3.08	14.06	7.78
484	18.50	0.00	0.00	10.02	5.50
485	12.08	3.07	4.10	17.06	8.90
486	15.06	3.19	4.00	13.05	8.00
487	14.01	3.00	4.04	13.09	7.85
488	14.00	2.45	4.04	12.11	7.70
489	13.29	2.52	4.06	16.02	8.20
490	16.77	4.16	3.06	11.05	7.70
491	15.06	3.26	3.08	13.00	7.85
492	14.42	3.14	4.04	13.05	7.60
493	14.14	3.25	3.10	13.08	7.50
494	14.25	2.47	4.04	14.05	8.30
495	12.09	2.55	4.10	15.06	10.65
496	13.02	2.40	4.06	14.03	6.00
497	13.97	2.37	4.02	12.11	8.00
498	16.17	3.10	3.06	12.00	8.45

Contd.

1	2	3	4	5	6
499	13.72	2.53	3.08	13.01	7.95
500	15.02	3.05	4.10	13.03	7.28
501	14.52	3.07	4.02	12.10	8.60
502	13.07	2.37	4.10	17.02	8.95
503	15.02	3.00	3.08	11.08	8.80
504	16.07	3.36	0.00	9.10	7.80
505	14.89	2.59	4.04	14.00	5.85
506	13.38	2.48	4.02	16.00	6.58
507	15.60	3.59	3.06	13.01	6.85
508	13.80	3.30	4.04	16.05	6.52
509	15.03	3.38	4.00	11.05	6.92
510	15.03	2.85	3.08	16.00	8.55
511	16.40	0.00	3.08	12.09	6.34
512	13.00	2.25	4.08	16.02	6.30
513	12.56	2.42	4.10	14.06	6.58
514	13.96	2.56	4.02	16.06	8.75
515	13.00	3.00	4.08	16.00	7.50
516	14.04	0.00	3.08	13.07	7.20
517	13.02	2.38	4.08	18.00	8.50
518	13.07	2.49	4.04	17.10	7.60
519	13.62	2.55	4.04	15.06	8.65
520	16.03	3.09	4.00	13.00	7.40
521	14.70	2.47	4.04	16.00	8.10
522	13.74	2.59	4.04	15.05	7.34
523	12.16	2.32	4.04	17.00	8.34
524	13.39	2.34	4.08	16.02	8.20
525	16.00	2.51	4.00	13.02	5.95
526	19.00	0.00	3.08	10.00	7.70
527	17.02	3.01	0.00	9.08	6.30
528	13.06	2.33	5.00	16.02	8.25
529	15.52	3.14	0.00	12.05	7.25
530	13.09	2.55	4.02	14.00	7.00

Contd.

1	2	3	4	5	6
531	16.01	3.53	3.08	10.07	6.20
532	14.00	3.00	4.04	14.00	8.55
533	15.01	3.10	3.06	12.00	7.21
534	14.96	2.41	3.10	13.05	6.30
535	13.77	2.45	4.00	15.06	6.81
536	14.28	0.00	3.10	14.09	7.08
537	14.00	2.55	4.02	15.08	7.32
538	16.00	3.37	3.06	11.02	6.00
539	13.08	2.42	4.06	14.00	7.00
540	13.44	2.50	4.04	16.11	9.75
541	15.84	3.39	3.08	11.10	6.35
542	13.62	3.06	4.02	15.00	8.35
543	14.05	2.49	4.06	16.00	6.60
544	14.01	3.10	4.06	14.02	8.70
545	15.06	3.22	3.10	13.04	6.70
546	14.14	2.50	4.00	14.10	8.10
547	12.89	2.35	4.10	16.01	7.80
548	12.10	2.51	5.02	17.07	8.90
549	14.00	3.05	3.06	15.02	9.40
550	12.99	2.44	4.04	16.00	8.40
551	13.16	3.05	4.04	15.00	8.40
552	14.07	3.10	3.06	14.00	5.80
553	15.04	3.34	3.06	13.06	7.55
554	14.31	2.47	3.10	15.07	7.70
555	13.84	2.52	4.10	15.04	7.60
556	13.82	3.02	4.06	14.00	8.80
557	14.87	3.35	0.00	14.05	8.40
558	13.92	2.56	3.06	14.04	6.70
559	12.91	2.44	3.10	15.03	9.70
560	14.94	2.41	4.00	14.07	6.50
561	13.07	2.51	4.08	14.04	9.60
562	14.03	3.13	4.10	13.03	9.00

Cont.

1	*2*	*3*	*4*	*5*	*6*
563	13.80	3.09	4.08	14.06	9.00
564	14.49	2.35	4.02	13.08	6.70
565	15.12	3.44	3.06	13.00	7.20
566	18.51	4.00	3.10	14.02	9.20
567	17.00	3.40	3.10	9.10	6.10
568	16.83	3.25	0.00	10.01	5.00
569	13.09	3.00	4.08	15.06	8.80
570	15.02	3.10	0.00	11.00	6.40
571	15.04	3.01	4.00	11.01	7.20
572	15.02	3.22	3.10	10.01	7.10
573	16.18	2.55	3.10	11.04	6.80
574	14.52	2.58	4.02	13.00	7.20
575	14.20	3.05	4.02	13.05	7.60
576	14.07	3.17	3.10	13.01	7.00
577	14.88	2.52	4.00	12.00	6.20
578	14.09	2.44	4.08	14.09	8.65
579	14.08	3.20	4.04	13.11	7.30
580	13.91	2.51	4.04	14.07	6.65
581	13.98	2.85	4.04	14.08	8.70
582	14.18	2.61	4.04	14.09	8.70
583	14.81	3.02	4.06	12.03	6.80
584	15.64	3.25	3.10	10.04	6.65
585	13.30	2.40	3.06	15.02	8.25
586	14.70	2.47	4.04	12.05	8.50
587	13.65	2.35	4.04	14.07	7.10
588	15.08	3.16	3.08	12.04	8.30
589	14.66	3.11	4.02	12.06	9.20
590	15.15	3.20	3.08	11.10	7.20
591	14.60	3.09	4.04	14.04	6.10
592	14.00	2.49	3.10	14.00	6.55
593	13.24	2.53	4.04	15.07	8.40
594	14.22	3.22	3.10	12.02	5.85

Contd.

1	2	3	4	5	6
595	13.91	2.39	4.08	14.06	9.00
596	12.69	2.21	4.02	14.05	7.20
597	13.07	2.40	4.10	16.00	8.25
598	14.03	2.56	4.00	14.02	6.05
599	12.56	2.26	4.10	15.02	8.15
600	13.75	2.32	4.10	15.02	7.20
601	15.34	3.00	0.00	10.07	6.20
602	13.08	3.20	4.10	13.06	7.70
603	14.59	2.49	4.00	13.03	7.50
604	13.47	2.49	4.00	14.06	7.10
605	13.00	2.43	3.06	16.08	8.70
606	14.07	3.20	0.00	13.09	7.20
607	12.07	2.18	4.04	14.07	6.70
608	13.35	2.47	0.00	14.08	7.45
609	14.13	3.01	4.00	14.06	7.10
610	12.78	2.35	4.10	17.00	8.60
611	13.08	2.59	4.06	14.03	8.00
612	14.96	3.23	3.08	13.00	6.50
613	12.06	2.42	5.00	16.07	8.90
614	13.17	2.33	4.06	17.01	8.10
615	13.00	3.11	3.10	11.08	6.00
616	16.03	3.35	3.10	14.02	8.10
617	16.01	4.01	4.02	12.11	6.90
618	14.04	2.55	4.06	15.02	9.85
619	14.45	3.10	4.06	16.02	9.70
620	15.19	3.05	0.00	12.00	7.75
621	14.06	3.11	3.10	14.00	9.70
622	13.74	2.38	4.04	16.04	8.70
623	14.39	2.57	4.04	15.00	8.40
624	12.76	2.20	5.00	18.00	10.80
625	13.08	2.48	4.00	14.06	6.20
626	12.71	2.27	4.02	17.02	7.70

Contd.

1	*2*	*3*	*4*	*5*	*6*
627	14.62	2.59	3.10	14.11	7.60
628	11.99	2.43	5.00	17.04	11.30
629	14.15	2.54	4.08	13.06	8.00
630	13.08	3.00	4.06	13.10	7.80
631	14.24	3.04	4.02	13.00	6.70
632	14.28	2.48	4.06	13.10	8.25
633	15.02	3.15	3.10	11.06	6.90
634	13.08	2.47	4.00	13.02	6.60
635	13.39	2.39	5.04	18.09	8.20
636	14.06	2.57	4.00	12.11	7.25
637	14.34	3.22	4.02	13.10	6.10
638	15.28	3.31	3.10	10.07	7.00
639	14.13	2.43	4.06	14.07	8.70
640	13.25	2.35	4.10	15.11	8.85
641	14.83	2.40	4.02	12.11	6.25
642	13.88	2.55	4.00	13.11	6.25
643	15.18	2.54	4.00	12.11	5.30
644	13.65	2.53	4.02	14.09	7.80
645	14.18	2.34	4.00	15.02	7.00
646	13.79	2.36	4.04	15.03	8.00
647	14.08	2.57	3.08	13.00	6.05
648	14.07	2.57	4.08	14.02	8.05
649	15.28	2.58	4.02	13.03	6.55
650	13.63	2.44	4.06	16.02	7.90
651	14.51	3.09	3.10	15.00	6.90
652	14.00	3.13	3.10	12.06	7.35
653	16.00	3.04	3.10	12.00	7.50
654	14.16	2.49	4.02	14.05	6.90
655	13.08	2.54	3.08	13.10	7.10
656	14.06	2.49	3.10	13.00	6.70
657	14.07	2.45	3.10	16.03	8.90
658	14.08	2.58	4.06	15.00	8.10

Contd.

1	*2*	*3*	*4*	*5*	*6*
659	13.63	2.41	4.02	16.09	7.62
660	14.06	2.15	4.08	16.05	10.40
661	13.09	2.50	4.00	16.02	6.80
662	14.07	3.00	4.08	14.08	10.70
663	14.31	2.46	4.06	14.04	6.50
664	14.07	3.07	3.06	15.00	7.80
665	15.19	0.00	4.04	14.00	8.60
666	13.00	2.17	4.06	16.00	7.95
667	13.02	2.42	4.08	14.00	8.00
668	14.03	3.01	3.10	14.00	8.05
669	15.09	2.58	4.08	15.00	7.80
670	15.05	3.07	4.02	13.04	6.90
671	14.50	3.00	4.08	14.00	6.60
672	13.00	2.36	3.10	15.00	7.15
673	14.02	3.11	4.06	14.00	6.70
674	15.02	3.25	3.08	13.05	9.80
675	13.65	3.00	4.04	16.08	10.35
676	13.03	3.20	3.08	13.00	8.10
677	14.07	2.58	3.08	13.00	7.40
678	13.45	2.30	4.02	13.00	6.90
679	14.05	3.02	4.00	14.00	6.40
680	14.03	2.56	4.02	14.00	7.60
681	13.25	2.48	4.04	15.00	9.00
682	14.02	3.02	4.06	13.04	7.55
683	14.99	3.12	4.00	12.11	7.65
684	12.00	2.38	4.06	16.05	7.95
685	13.16	2.52	4.04	15.02	7.30
686	15.11	3.04	3.10	11.05	5.00
687	15.01	3.08	4.00	11.06	6.35
688	14.05	2.40	4.00	14.08	7.35
689	13.68	2.42	4.08	15.09	8.35
690	13.02	2.59	4.02	16.00	6.10

Contd.

1	*2*	*3*	*4*	*5*	*6*
691	14.21	3.25	4.02	15.06	9.25
692	13.64	3.00	4.02	12.05	9.65
693	14.05	3.01	3.10	13.00	9.00
694	14.07	3.06	3.10	14.04	5.65
695	13.84	2.52	4.08	15.06	9.85
696	14.33	2.48	4.08	14.06	8.45
697	14.00	2.56	4.02	16.04	10.10
698	15.24	3.03	0.00	13.06	6.25
699	14.41	3.00	4.02	13.06	8.90
700	13.03	2.29	4.02	16.04	8.15
701	15.09	3.30	4.06	12.00	9.45
702	14.02	3.15	3.08	13.06	6.55
703	14.03	3.09	3.10	12.00	6.55
704	14.70	2.56	3.08	13.03	8.23
705	14.81	3.05	0.00	13.06	7.30
706	15.04	2.57	4.02	13.05	6.55
707	14.70	3.18	4.02	14.09	9.15
708	14.21	2.43	5.00	15.04	7.40
709	15.08	3.06	3.10	12.06	7.30
710	14.98	3.01	3.06	13.10	9.00
711	14.07	3.10	3.10	15.00	4.80
712	14.09	3.55	3.08	16.02	8.85
713	15.00	3.32	4.02	16.01	9.90
714	14.02	2.41	3.10	15.02	7.35
715	14.00	4.32	4.00	13.05	9.90
716	14.35	2.44	4.00	14.03	6.90
717	13.03	2.46	4.02	15.09	6.61
718	13.19	2.42	4.06	16.02	8.20
719	15.44	3.46	4.00	15.03	8.10
720	14.09	3.30	3.06	11.00	5.59
721	15.00	2.56	3.10	13.05	5.91
722	13.00	2.50	4.02	15.04	7.24

Contd.

1	2	3	4	5	6
723	15.02	3.44	4.02	12.08	5.79
724	14.06	3.10	4.02	14.07	9.12
725	15.00	3.06	4.04	12.09	7.12
726	12.08	2.37	4.04	15.07	9.00
727	12.06	2.36	4.10	16.09	7.27
728	13.04	2.43	4.00	14.06	8.13
729	13.08	3.10	4.02	15.08	8.30
730	14.00	3.11	4.02	14.09	7.27
731	13.04	3.03	3.10	13.06	7.74
732	13.06	3.12	4.00	13.02	7.97
733	14.02	2.59	4.02	14.08	7.21
734	14.00	3.34	4.00	13.01	6.93
735	13.04	3.22	3.06	11.11	6.29
736	14.05	3.11	3.10	13.06	6.40
737	12.00	2.31	4.06	18.02	8.05
738	14.68	3.53	4.02	12.08	6.76
739	14.02	2.49	4.02	13.05	5.96
740	13.04	2.30	4.06	13.08	6.95
741	13.06	2.48	4.08	13.10	7.27
742	12.04	2.55	4.08	15.08	8.00
743	13.02	2.42	4.08	15.07	7.03
744	15.09	3.50	3.10	10.00	7.30
745	13.08	3.59	4.08	14.03	10.09
746	15.01	3.43	3.10	13.11	8.50
747	15.69	3.59	3.10	12.00	6.46
748	13.90	3.01	3.10	13.11	6.58
749	13.03	3.30	4.08	14.02	8.04
750	14.06	3.39	4.06	12.07	7.84
751	16.05	3.03	3.10	10.06	5.55
752	13.04	2.37	4.06	14.08	7.40
753	14.06	4.02	3.10	10.03	4.81
754	13.03	2.27	4.06	14.02	7.66

Contd.

1	2	3	4	5	6
755	13.02	2.43	4.04	13.04	9.94
756	13.00	2.26	4.06	13.10	7.40
757	14.00	3.07	3.10	13.04	6.15
758	13.02	2.43	3.10	13.00	6.75
759	13.00	3.06	4.04	13.00	6.14
760	14.01	2.51	4.00	13.00	6.05
761	13.30	3.06	4.06	13.10	7.35
762	12.05	2.40	4.02	13.11	7.95
763	14.06	3.03	4.00	13.02	6.60
764	14.08	3.01	4.00	12.10	7.45
765	12.03	3.04	4.08	15.09	8.80
766	13.05	2.51	4.00	13.06	7.07
767	12.08	2.31	4.06	15.07	8.56
768	14.00	2.40	4.02	14.02	7.07
769	13.06	2.42	4.06	13.00	8.50
770	13.06	2.50	4.00	14.05	7.16
771	15.08	4.00	3.08	10.07	6.45
772	14.06	3.05	4.00	13.01	6.00
773	13.06	3.25	4.00	14.05	9.34
774	13.08	2.39	4.02	14.06	10.82
775	14.05	3.26	4.00	13.03	6.09
776	13.03	2.39	3.10	14.07	6.17
777	14.09	3.24	0.00	12.01	6.27
778	12.90	3.02	4.04	12.11	7.97
779	13.03	2.48	3.10	11.03	6.67
780	14.04	2.50	4.04	14.02	7.04
781	14.08	3.15	3.10	12.04	5.50
782	13.07	2.46	4.08	13.10	7.82
783	13.03	2.49	4.04	14.07	7.68
784	15.04	3.52	3.10	12.00	7.72
785	14.00	3.58	4.08	10.02	7.05
786	13.06	2.59	4.08	14.09	9.10

Contd

1	2	3	4	5	6
787	15.05	2.50	0.00	12.02	6.43
788	11.08	2.50	4.10	16.06	10.35
789	13.04	3.00	3.10	14.03	7.15
790	14.00	4.01	0.00	10.01	5.10
791	14.00	3.23	4.00	11.08	7.43
792	16.05	2.49	0.00	0.00	6.95
793	14.00	2.51	4.00	13.05	9.01
794	14.08	3.47	3.10	10.06	7.10
795	14.00	3.40	4.00	13.07	8.22
796	14.00	3.25	4.00	13.10	8.53
797	14.03	3.25	4.00	13.08	10.13
798	12.09	2.59	4.06	16.00	10.49
799	13.03	3.10	4.08	13.04	9.80
800	14.00	3.10	4.00	13.05	8.60
801	13.09	2.41	4.06	14.09	8.50
802	12.08	2.33	4.03	16.06	9.40
803	12.04	2.42	4.10	15.05	9.95
804	15.02	3.03	4.00	11.09	7.00
805	14.00	3.00	4.00	13.10	7.30
806	13.04	2.49	4.03	15.02	8.80
807	14.00	3.13	3.06	13.10	8.80
808	14.02	2.50	4.00	12.06	9.47
809	14.00	2.51	4.00	13.02	8.50
810	14.02	3.04	3.10	12.09	7.00
811	12.09	2.48	4.00	13.03	9.00
812	14.00	3.12	4.00	13.01	7.30
813	13.00	2.37	4.02	15.00	9.93
814	13.00	3.00	4.04	13.08	8.00
815	15.00	3.44	4.00	13.01	7.52
816	15.02	3.34	4.02	13.09	9.00
817	13.06	2.31	4.00	13.05	8.30
818	13.05	2.32	4.00	14.04	8.69

Contd.

1	*2*	*3*	*4*	*5*	*6*
819	13.08	2.59	4.06	13.09	8.36
820	15.03	3.43	4.00	12.00	7.50
821	13.06	3.13	4.08	14.03	8.65
822	13.00	2.42	4.00	13.08	8.85
823	13.00	2.40	4.00	13.00	8.85
824	13.02	3.07	4.08	13.06	10.10
825	15.02	3.09	4.00	11.05	6.94
826	14.00	2.51	0.00	11.10	7.10
827	15.02	3.18	4.08	10.10	7.00
828	14.02	2.48	4.00	13.02	8.55
829	13.02	2.42	4.04	15.03	9.33
830	13.03	2.33	4.02	15.05	8.72
831	13.00	2.56	4.04	14.02	8.15
832	13.04	2.35	4.00	13.03	8.45
833	14.03	3.26	4.00	13.02	8.45
834	14.06	3.10	4.02	11.05	6.40
835	13.01	3.06	4.04	14.06	8.73
836	15.00	3.05	4.04	12.05	9.58
837	14.01	2.44	4.04	13.08	7.72
838	13.50	2.41	3.06	12.00	7.95
839	14.06	3.12	4.00	13.01	7.00
840	13.05	2.59	4.04	15.09	8.85
841	13.03	2.46	4.04	13.08	8.30
842	12.06	2.36	4.06	13.08	9.20
843	12.08	2.49	4.00	14.00	7.70
844	12.01	2.28	4.10	15.02	12.00
845	13.05	3.35	4.20	12.06	8.36
846	15.05	3.25	3.06	11.04	7.42
847	14.00	3.05	4.02	12.07	7.95
848	14.01	2.31	4.02	12.07	8.00
849	13.47	2.45	4.04	16.01	17.35
850	14.00	2.57	4.02	14.07	7.20

Contd.

1	2	3	4	5	6
851	13.00	2.47	4.02	13.05	7.10
852	15.05	2.40	3.08	10.06	8.40
853	14.56	3.01	4.00	14.08	6.39
854	14.01	3.05	4.02	12.02	6.30
855	13.09	2.39	4.06	13.08	7.76
856	13.02	2.33	4.08	16.04	9.04
857	15.19	2.42	4.00	11.01	8.60
858	14.05	3.04	4.02	12.10	8.74
859	15.01	3.50	3.10	11.03	8.32
860	16.06	0.00	3.10	10.02	8.12
861	15.05	2.49	3.08	11.03	6.10
862	14.09	3.20	4.00	13.04	7.10
863	14.00	3.09	4.02	12.11	7.72
864	13.07	2.38	4.08	14.02	7.60
865	13.08	2.55	5.00	16.03	8.10
866	12.73	2.30	4.02	15.01	7.64
867	12.04	2.55	4.10	15.03	8.00
868	14.05	3.13	3.06	12.01	6.04
869	13.07	3.00	4.02	12.02	7.80
870	13.03	3.08	3.08	12.06	4.82
871	12.31	2.36	5.00	17.02	8.60
872	14.43	3.04	4.02	12.01	7.66
873	14.01	3.00	4.02	14.05	8.34
874	13.02	2.38	4.04	15.02	7.91
875	16.09	3.25	3.06	0.00	5.55
876	13.08	2.53	4.08	16.05	9.86
877	15.08	3.30	3.08	12.06	6.46
878	14.54	3.05	3.10	11.09	9.29
879	14.03	2.43	4.00	11.09	6.85
880	13.03	2.46	4.06	16.00	8.88
881	14.09	3.13	4.04	13.03	6.46
882	14.34	3.14	4.04	11.00	6.54

Contd.

1	*2*	*3*	*4*	*5*	*6*
883	15.01	3.09	4.00	11.09	6.14
884	16.07	0.00	0.00	10.06	6.08
885	13.02	2.53	4.10	14.03	8.51
886	13.08	3.11	5.02	13.09	8.35
887	14.47	2.52	4.04	14.03	7.48
888	13.04	2.45	4.02	14.05	8.51
889	13.05	2.56	4.08	13.07	9.10
890	16.03	3.36	3.10	10.06	3.85
891	14.01	2.52	4.06	15.04	7.40
892	14.05	3.03	4.04	12.04	9.13
893	13.09	2.52	4.08	14.09	8.37
894	16.09	4.12	3.10	0.00	6.47
895	14.50	2.54	4.06	13.00	8.21
896	14.50	2.47	0.00	13.03	5.01
897	15.03	2.56	3.10	13.00	5.45
898	14.00	3.04	4.02	13.05	7.60
899	12.09	2.23	4.06	15.09	7.50
900	15.02	0.00	4.02	12.03	7.76
901	15.34	3.05	0.00	13.10	6.80
902	15.03	3.09	0.00	10.08	8.14
903	12.07	2.26	4.02	14.04	6.52
904	14.02	3.18	4.06	13.10	7.44
905	12.93	2.34	4.06	15.03	6.60
906	13.00	2.23	4.08	15.09	7.62
907	14.06	0.00	0.00	0.00	5.70
908	13.04	2.13	4.10	15.02	8.28
909	15.04	2.49	4.00	11.11	6.30
910	13.07	2.57	4.10	15.04	6.92
911	14.00	3.06	4.04	12.08	8.32
912	12.09	2.32	4.04	14.07	7.12
913	14.00	3.01	4.02	13.01	7.80
914	13.02	2.50	4.06	14.00	7.70

Contd.

1	*2*	*3*	*4*	*5*	*6*
915	13.09	3.09	3.10	12.11	7.72
916	14.05	3.44	4.02	10.07	6.50
917	15.00	4.26	4.04	12.03	8.20
918	15.02	3.00	4.00	12.03	6.65
919	14.05	3.14	4.02	12.04	5.70
920	13.01	2.56	4.10	14.06	8.00
921	14.01	3.30	3.08	11.10	5.92
922	12.38	2.58	4.00	12.05	8.65
923	13.00	2.39	4.02	13.03	7.06
924	14.00	2.36	4.02	14.01	7.84
925	14.00	3.08	3.10	13.10	6.94
926	14.38	2.53	4.00	14.03	7.36
927	14.09	3.13	3.08	12.01	6.90
928	15.50	4.07	4.00	11.05	7.48
929	14.06	3.05	3.08	11.06	6.45
930	14.06	3.07	3.10	13.01	6.70
931	14.08	3.58	4.00	10.05	7.64
932	15.62	3.27	4.00	11.07	7.90
933	15.04	0.00	0.00	0.00	5.46
934	16.00	3.50	0.00	11.05	7.90
935	13.04	3.32	4.06	14.07	9.16
936	13.02	2.29	4.00	14.07	7.20
937	11.08	2.35	4.00	15.10	8.24
938	12.31	2.21	4.06	17.08	7.50
939	13.03	2.42	4.06	10.08	8.23
940	13.38	2.57	4.08	16.02	8.56
941	13.06	2.51	4.02	14.02	7.94
942	15.01	4.26	4.02	11.03	7.24
943	15.06	3.43	3.10	12.04	6.56
944	15.07	3.35	3.08	10.11	6.80
945	13.70	2.51	4.04	14.08	9.99
946	13.05	2.57	4.10	14.08	7.59

Contd.

1	*2*	*3*	*4*	*5*	*6*
947	14.05	3.24	4.00	13.00	7.74
948	16.01	3.56	4.00	11.10	7.09
949	13.50	2.58	4.00	13.04	8.13
950	19.00	4.02	3.08	10.03	6.94
951	15.40	3.47	4.00	11.06	8.22
952	13.08	3.26	4.02	14.06	10.49
953	15.00	3.15	4.00	11.08	8.74
954	14.08	3.05	4.00	12.06	7.07
955	19.16	4.38	3.08	0.00	6.25
956	15.07	3.08	3.06	12.03	7.20
957	13.40	2.33	5.00	14.00	8.42
958	13.60	3.17	4.10	12.02	9.04
959	14.82	2.42	4.00	13.07	7.66
960	14.02	3.05	3.10	11.05	5.59
961	14.00	2.41	4.00	14.01	8.21
962	14.08	3.33	4.00	13.10	6.92
963	15.59	2.58	4.04	12.10	6.99
964	14.02	2.42	4.04	13.06	6.85
965	13.08	2.49	4.04	13.05	8.30
966	13.01	2.53	4.02	16.06	8.00
967	15.09	0.00	4.02	11.05	6.90
968	13.06	2.53	4.04	14.12	5.95
969	12.08	2.53	4.10	15.04	8.85
970	13.00	2.40	4.02	16.05	7.60
971	13.09	2.43	4.06	15.05	6.20
972	12.08	2.36	4.04	14.09	7.30
973	13.00	3.21	4.08	16.00	7.90
974	13.00	2.45	4.10	15.02	10.30
975	14.04	3.37	4.04	13.01	7.70
976	12.09	3.06	4.08	14.05	7.46
977	13.05	2.45	4.04	13.12	7.17
978	13.06	3.37	4.02	12.05	6.70

Contd.

1	*2*	*3*	*4*	*5*	*6*
979	13.02	2.53	4.08	12.08	6.72
980	14.18	3.07	4.04	13.05	6.82
981	14.00	3.12	4.04	14.09	7.71
982	13.05	2.52	4.10	14.08	7.55
983	15.03	2.51	4.06	13.02	8.30
984	13.08	3.07	4.10	16.04	8.48
985	15.09	3.02	3.08	11.10	6.20
986	13.02	2.40	4.00	14.06	8.50
987	14.05	2.57	4.04	13.00	6.85
988	14.19	3.01	4.02	12.01	6.85
989	13.65	3.31	4.08	13.03	9.38
990	14.02	3.06	4.08	14.09	7.55
991	12.03	2.44	4.10	15.04	7.82
992	16.01	3.58	3.10	10.07	6.28
993	14.08	3.21	0.00	10.03	6.57
994	14.02	3.10	4.02	12.08	6.85
995	13.05	3.00	4.04	13.04	7.25
996	15.03	3.14	3.10	11.03	5.47
997	14.06	0.00	3.08	12.10	0.00
998	16.09	3.35	0.00	10.07	5.65
999	15.00	3.07	4.00	11.10	8.52
1000	14.05	3.00	4.04	11.07	5.00
1001	12.06	3.07	4.08	15.09	8.45
1002	14.00	3.28	4.02	13.03	6.25
1003	14.04	2.55	4.02	11.11	6.45
1004	14.06	3.40	4.00	11.11	8.97
1005	15.28	2.54	4.04	12.08	6.28
1006	13.07	2.56	4.02	15.06	8.13
1007	17.08	4.09	0.00	10.07	8.50
1008	12.04	2.19	4.10	16.09	6.93
1009	12.00	2.41	5.00	18.05	9.40
1010	13.00	3.45	5.00	18.02	9.95

Contd.

1	*2*	*3*	*4*	*5*	*6*
1011	13.34	2.59	3.10	14.05	8.51
1012	13.22	3.08	4.02	13.02	7.55
1013	13.06	3.04	4.02	14.03	8.25
1014	15.05	0.00	3.06	11.07	8.18
1015	15.04	3.13	4.00	12.03	7.05
1016	14.06	3.34	4.00	13.02	6.25
1017	12.05	3.00	3.10	13.09	6.65
1018	13.54	3.10	4.06	14.06	8.40
1019	13.05	2.41	3.10	15.00	9.90
1020	14.04	3.10	4.06	14.10	7.50
1021	15.00	3.45	3.10	12.11	7.00
1022	15.02	3.34	0.00	11.06	5.80
1023	14.05	3.09	3.10	11.06	6.57
1024	13.08	2.55	3.10	14.07	8.65
1025	14.04	3.51	3.08	13.05	8.40
1026	12.09	2.21	3.08	14.03	6.55
1027	11.02	2.36	4.08	15.08	9.54
1028	13.02	2.42	3.08	15.02	7.58
1029	12.53	2.34	4.06	15.02	8.94
1030	13.07	2.32	3.08	16.05	8.93
1031	13.03	2.35	4.06	14.05	5.73
1032	15.05	3.12	0.00	11.11	5.89
1033	16.00	0.00	0.00	11.00	4.71
1034	14.08	3.06	3.08	11.09	7.70
1035	13.09	2.45	3.06	13.02	7.55
1036	13.09	2.45	4.02	13.11	7.39
1037	0.00	0.00	4.00	13.06	9.64
1038	14.97	0.00	0.00	11.04	7.35
1039	14.31	2.55	3.10	13.07	7.97
1040	13.04	2.51	4.02	14.07	8.35
1041	13.04	2.44	3.08	15.06	8.21
1042	13.05	3.01	4.02	13.07	6.90

Contd.

1	*2*	*3*	*4*	*5*	*6*
1043	14.00	2.45	4.06	14.00	7.45
1044	14.04	3.47	3.10	11.10	6.86
1045	15.35	0.00	4.00	12.07	7.87
1046	15.09	0.00	0.00	11.00	7.49
1047	12.07	2.22	3.06	12.05	7.06
1048	14.01	2.43	3.06	13.07	7.75
1049	13.08	3.10	3.10	12.09	7.83
1050	15.02	3.38	3.08	12.07	8.64
1051	13.02	2.59	4.00	12.08	7.42
1052	12.07	2.36	5.00	15.06	7.03
1053	13.32	0.00	3.10	12.02	7.46
1054	13.56	2.42	3.08	13.02	8.80
1055	15.03	3.47	3.06	10.10	8.24
1056	14.00	3.02	3.06	14.01	9.79
1057	14.00	3.15	3.06	14.00	9.43
1058	13.06	3.05	4.04	14.05	10.49
1059	14.09	3.33	4.04	11.06	7.81

APPENDIX-2

PECET-PHYSICAL EFFICIENCY TEST RAW SCORES (WOMEN)

S.No.	100M	800M	High	Long	Shot
1	19.00	1.40	1.07	3.10	5.40
2	27.00	2.10	1.07	1.63	3.39
3	15.08	1.50	1.09	2.84	5.62
4	19.00	1.58	1.24	2.84	5.40
5	15.60	1.28	1.19	2.74	5.57
6	18.60	1.35	1.14	2.82	5.13
7	15.80	1.15	1.32	2.84	4.95
8	15.00	1.30	1.19	2.69	6.20
9	16.20	1.19	1.07	2.92	5.45
10	19.50	1.39	1.07	2.26	4.00
11	19.20	1.45	1.30	2.51	5.77
12	23.00	1.50	1.07	2.44	4.79
13	17.20	1.37	1.09	3.30	5.04
14	24.00	2.00	1.07	1.83	3.71
15	18.40	1.35	1.19	3.10	3.80
16	16.50	1.24	1.09	3.45	6.24
17	18.00	1.48	1.09	3.18	6.08
18	16.10	1.15	1.35	3.10	6.90

Contd.

1	2	3	4	5	6
19	16.20	1.25	1.24	3.05	5.83
20	14.80	1.15	1.24	3.33	8.45
21	15.40	1.08	1.24	3.73	5.62
22	17.10	1.36	1.14	2.79	5.50
23	17.00	1.22	1.19	3.35	5.71
24	16.00	1.21	1.09	3.78	5.83
25	19.00	1.44	1.09	2.54	3.74
26	20.00	2.05	1.09	3.30	4.37
27	17.30	1.29	1.09	3.30	4.89
28	17.50	1.28	1.09	3.02	4.98
29	17.00	1.28	1.09	2.95	5.12
30	15.90	1.17	1.24	3.73	5.72
31	19.50	1.39	1.07	2.26	4.00
32	16.70	1.39	1.07	3.23	8.15
33	20.00	2.31	1.07	2.18	3.70
34	19.00	1.40	1.07	3.10	5.40
35	19.20	1.45	1.30	2.51	5.77
36	14.80	1.15	1.24	3.33	8.45
37	15.40	1.08	1.24	3.73	5.62
38	17.10	1.36	1.14	2.79	5.50
39	18.10	1.35	1.24	3.05	6.24
40	17.40	1.35	1.09	3.33	5.10
41	16.10	1.32	1.19	3.38	5.66
42	15.80	1.20	1.09	3.10	4.36
43	16.80	1.27	1.09	3.15	4.14
44	15.10	1.18	1.24	3.51	6.01
45	27.00	2.10	1.07	1.63	3.39
46	17.00	1.28	1.09	2.95	5.12
47	15.90	1.17	1.24	3.73	5.72
48	19.50	1.39	1.07	2.26	4.00
49	16.70	1.39	1.07	3.23	8.15
50	17.00	1.22	1.19	3.35	5.71

Contd.

1	*2*	*3*	*4*	*5*	*6*
51	16.00	1.21	1.09	3.78	5.83
52	19.00	1.44	1.09	2.54	3.74
53	23.00	1.50	1.07	2.44	4.79
54	19.40	1.47	1.14	2.41	4.62
55	21.00	2.10	1.04	2.08	6.20
56	14.00	1.17	1.19	3.66	6.59
57	16.03	1.33	1.09	3.28	6.51
58	16.01	1.32	1.09	2.90	5.00
59	17.20	1.37	1.09	3.30	5.04
60	20.00	2.05	1.09	3.30	4.37
61	17.30	1.29	1.09	3.30	4.89
62	17.50	1.28	1.09	3.02	4.98
63	16.10	1.32	1.19	3.38	5.66
64	15.80	1.20	1.09	3.10	4.36
65	16.80	1.27	1.09	3.15	4.14
66	15.10	1.18	1.24	3.51	6.01
67	20.00	2.31	1.07	2.18	3.70
68	19.00	1.40	1.07	3.10	5.40
69	19.20	1.45	1.30	2.51	5.77
70	14.80	1.15	1.24	3.33	8.45
71	15.08	1.50	1.09	2.84	5.62
72	24.00	2.00	1.07	1.83	3.71
73	27.00	2.10	1.07	1.63	3.39
74	17.00	1.28	1.09	2.95	5.12
75	15.90	1.17	1.24	3.73	5.72
76	19.50	1.39	1.07	2.26	4.00
77	18.80	1.48	1.04	2.44	5.73
78	17.00	2.19	1.07	2.49	6.40
79	20.00	1.49	1.04	2.62	5.59
80	18.07	1.34	1.14	2.59	4.50
81	15.48	1.42	1.09	3.71	6.02
82	19.00	1.54	1.14	3.05	5.65

Contd.

1	2	3	4	5	6
83	19.08	1.45	1.04	2.39	4.01
84	18.40	1.35	1.19	3.10	3.80
85	15.40	1.08	1.24	3.73	5.62
86	17.10	1.36	1.14	2.79	5.50
87	19.00	1.58	1.24	2.84	5.40
88	18.10	1.35	1.24	3.05	6.24
89	17.40	1.35	1.09	3.33	5.10
90	18.02	2.11	1.04	2.72	5.75
91	23.07	2.01	1.14	2.87	5.90
92	17.00	1.38	1.14	3.20	6.40
93	15.00	1.15	1.09	3.45	5.30
94	19.00	1.53	1.04	2.13	3.91
95	16.50	1.24	1.09	3.45	6.24
96	16.70	1.39	1.07	3.23	8.15
97	17.00	1.22	1.19	3.35	5.71
98	16.00	1.21	1.09	3.78	5.83
99	19.00	1.44	1.09	2.54	3.74
100	16.90	1.44	1.14	2.49	5.40
101	15.60	1.28	1.19	2.74	5.57
102	18.00	1.48	1.09	3.18	6.08
103	16.10	1.15	1.35	3.10	6.90
104	16.20	1.25	1.24	3.05	5.83
105	16.05	1.40	1.19	3.35	5.50
106	17.03	1.31	1.19	3.18	5.44
107	15.03	1.30	1.09	3.56	6.92
108	15.80	1.54	1.04	2.87	6.02
109	15.90	1.50	1.12	2.21	4.32
110	15.80	1.40	1.30	3.78	6.75
111	18.60	1.35	1.14	2.82	5.13
112	16.50	2.43	1.04	3.25	4.80
113	15.10	1.20	1.30	3.15	5.50
114	19.10	1.32	1.04	2.69	5.15

Contd.

1	*2*	*3*	*4*	*5*	*6*
115	17.00	1.53	1.14	3.07	4.95
116	15.30	1.23	1.27	3.28	0.67
117	31.00	2.45	1.04	2.08	4.01
118	16.10	1.50	1.14	3.00	8.00
119	23.06	2.46	1.04	2.11	3.81
120	19.00	1.52	1.07	2.67	4.67
121	15.80	1.15	1.32	2.84	4.95
122	14.50	1.20	1.09	3.35	7.67
123	17.50	1.30	1.07	2.16	4.87
124	17.02	2.36	1.30	3.28	4.45
125	15.80	1.24	1.24	3.51	5.93
126	18.01	1.27	1.19	2.90	5.90
127	18.00	2.20	1.07	2.29	4.95
128	17.08	1.38	1.09	3.20	4.02
129	16.20	1.32	1.14	3.23	5.06
130	23.00	1.52	1.07	1.70	3.00
131	15.03	1.14	1.30	3.40	6.08
132	15.00	1.30	1.19	2.69	6.20
133	19.00	1.41	1.14	2.74	3.97
134	23.20	2.40	1.07	1.32	3.10
135	19.80	1.47	1.07	2.08	4.70
136	15.20	1.21	1.30	2.49	6.85
137	17.50	1.42	1.09	2.82	4.90
138	23.60	1.38	1.14	2.16	5.85
139	19.00	1.54	1.07	2.21	5.67
140	17.70	1.30	1.07	3.15	5.09
141	16.20	1.19	1.07	2.92	5.45
142	16.10	1.24	1.09	2.54	4.50
143	16.50	1.32	1.19	3.02	5.70
144	15.60	1.40	1.14	3.30	5.95
145	24.00	2.14	1.14	2.90	5.76
146	16.30	1.24	1.19	3.56	5.92

Contd.

1	*2*	*3*	*4*	*5*	*6*
147	20.00	1.46	1.07	2.49	4.30
148	15.10	1.27	1.30	3.86	6.51
149	16.80	1.20	1.35	3.38	6.34
150	15.00	1.14	1.24	3.96	7.22
151	23.00	2.09	1.04	1.22	3.65
152	17.20	1.45	1.19	3.15	6.15
153	15.60	1.20	1.19	3.48	5.01
154	16.00	1.35	1.09	2.74	6.21
155	16.60	1.45	1.14	3.53	6.80
156	15.00	1.17	1.35	2.41	6.20
157	17.00	1.39	1.40	3.05	6.26
158	22.00	2.00	1.07	2.69	4.72
159	18.25	1.54	0.89	2.64	4.53
160	18.00	2.10	0.79	2.90	3.07
161	19.00	2.08	0.99	2.87	6.31
162	21.50	2.23	0.91	2.54	4.85
163	20.35	2.00	1.14	2.51	4.69
164	17.50	1.33	0.99	3.07	4.33
165	16.50	1.36	1.07	3.33	5.56
166	17.60	1.49	0.99	2.72	4.79
167	18.60	1.44	0.86	2.24	5.00
168	17.50	1.27	0.99	3.35	5.00
169	19.40	2.12	0.94	2.72	4.48
170	23.00	2.13	0.00	2.16	3.64
171	19.20	1.52	0.86	2.59	5.15
172	20.81	1.55	0.81	2.44	3.19
173	16.50	1.32	1.19	3.02	5.70
174	15.60	1.40	1.14	3.30	5.95
175	24.00	2.14	1.14	2.90	5.76
176	16.30	1.24	1.19	3.56	5.92
177	17.20	1.42	0.86	2.36	5.32
178	16.50	1.36	1.17	3.25	5.46

Contd.

1	*2*	*3*	*4*	*5*	*6*
179	19.50	2.06	0.97	2.34	3.77
180	19.10	1.51	0.81	2.51	3.52
181	19.10	2.10	0.76	2.16	3.93
182	17.50	2.10	0.76	2.41	4.74
183	19.30	1.37	0.91	2.18	5.23
184	17.06	1.47	0.81	2.34	5.81
185	20.10	1.58	0.76	2.39	3.20
186	16.50	1.41	0.86	2.90	5.31
187	20.00	1.46	1.07	2.49	4.30
188	15.10	1.27	1.30	3.86	6.51
189	16.80	1.20	1.35	3.38	6.34
190	15.00	1.14	1.24	3.96	7.22
191	21.00	2.11	0.76	2.13	4.42
192	15.90	1.49	1.02	2.95	5.43
193	19.80	2.15	0.81	2.84	5.74
194	18.50	1.47	1.02	2.51	4.40
195	15.80	1.43	0.97	3.10	5.42
196	18.10	1.50	1.07	2.44	3.61
197	16.00	1.50	1.27	3.25	5.75
198	18.00	1.33	1.02	3.28	5.50
199	16.20	1.24	1.27	3.28	5.73
200	23.00	2.09	1.04	1.22	3.65
201	17.20	1.45	1.19	3.15	6.15
202	15.60	1.20	1.19	3.48	5.01
203	16.00	1.35	1.09	2.74	6.21
204	17.56	1.44	1.22	3.02	5.00
205	17.00	1.47	1.12	3.30	6.69
206	18.50	1.48	1.09	3.02	6.71
207	17.50	1.34	1.12	3.23	6.20
208	15.20	1.41	1.22	2.95	5.95
209	16.00	1.40	0.91	2.87	4.85
210	16.00	1.50	1.07	2.95	6.20

Contd.

1	2	3	4	5	6
211	17.00	1.26	1.09	3.20	6.42
212	17.00	1.37	1.22	3.40	6.70
213	23.00	2.40	0.76	2.18	4.00
214	17.50	1.36	1.02	3.15	5.70
215	17.00	1.57	1.02	2.62	4.73
216	18.90	2.34	1.02	2.84	5.62
217	14.80	1.32	1.02	3.45	6.00
218	14.90	1.30	1.19	3.51	6.37
219	17.00	1.37	1.12	2.67	5.13
220	17.80	2.10	0.81	3.05	5.29
221	19.00	2.08	1.02	3.07	5.39
222	17.00	1.39	0.97	3.40	3.92
223	15.90	1.36	0.97	3.00	5.94
224	18.00	1.56	0.97	3.00	6.48
225	16.50	1.38	1.02	3.30	5.60
226	22.65	1.51	0.97	2.31	4.69
227	18.25	1.54	0.89	2.64	4.53
228	18.00	2.10	0.79	2.90	3.07
229	19.00	2.08	0.99	2.87	6.31
230	21.50	2.23	0.91	2.54	4.85
231	16.10	1.32	1.19	3.38	5.66
232	15.80	1.20	1.09	3.10	4.36
233	16.80	1.27	1.09	3.15	4.14
234	15.10	1.18	1.24	3.51	6.01
235	16.01	1.30	1.02	3.48	7.50
236	16.50	1.21	1.07	3.53	6.15
237	18.90	1.39	0.97	2.67	5.55
238	17.28	1.30	0.91	3.25	4.70
239	25.50	2.40	1.02	1.98	4.80
240	16.00	1.31	1.07	3.66	5.10
241	14.90	1.20	0.97	3.89	7.80
242	17.12	1.33	1.07	3.99	6.50

Contd.

1	*2*	*3*	*4*	*5*	*6*
243	22.29	2.10	0.91	2.87	5.50
244	20.35	2.00	1.14	2.51	4.69
245	17.50	1.33	0.99	3.07	4.33
246	16.50	1.36	1.07	3.33	5.56
247	17.60	1.49	0.99	2.72	4.79
248	18.60	1.44	0.86	2.24	5.00
249	27.00	2.10	1.07	1.63	3.39
250	17.00	1.28	1.09	2.95	5.12
251	15.90	1.17	1.24	3.73	5.72
252	19.50	1.39	1.07	2.26	4.00
253	17.50	1.27	0.99	3.35	5.00
254	[illegible]	2.12	0.94	2.72	4.48
255	[illegible]	2.13	1.07	2.16	3.64
256	19.20	1.52	0.86	2.59	5.15
257	19.90	1.43	0.91	2.82	4.10
258	17.70	1.54	1.07	3.10	6.20
259	17.55	1.28	0.91	3.51	4.75
260	16.10	1.32	1.19	3.38	5.66
261	15.80	1.20	1.09	3.10	4.36
262	16.80	1.27	1.09	3.15	4.14
263	15.10	1.18	1.24	3.51	6.01
264	18.04	1.37	0.97	3.89	6.45
265	20.00	2.30	1.07	2.21	3.10
266	18.00	1.40	0.91	3.43	5.00
267	19.05	1.30	0.76	2.49	5.20
268	18.88	1.50	1.09	3.05	5.40
269	17.00	1.32	1.12	3.35	4.80
270	23.90	1.57	0.91	2.74	4.75
271	23.36	2.05	1.02	2.67	9.00
272	15.28	1.45	1.07	3.23	6.00
273	17.37	1.35	0.76	3.10	5.70
274	20.81	1.55	0.81	2.44	3.19

Contd.

1	2	3	4	5	6
275	17.20	1.42	0.86	2.36	5.32
276	16.50	1.36	1.17	3.25	5.46
277	17.50	2.10	0.76	2.41	4.74
278	19.30	1.37	0.91	2.18	5.23
279	17.06	1.47	0.81	2.39	5.81
280	20.10	1.58	0.76	2.39	3.20
281	17.65	1.29	1.07	3.40	4.75
282	22.10	2.04	0.91	2.51	4.50
283	15.82	1.36	1.12	3.66	4.85
284	21.46	1.57	0.91	2.29	5.10
285	20.90	1.35	0.97	3.58	5.60
286	16.01	1.30	1.02	3.48	7.50
287	16.50	1.21	1.07	3.53	6.15
288	18.90	1.39	0.97	2.67	5.55
289	17.28	1.30	0.91	3.25	4.70
290	19.70	1.33	0.86	2.95	5.15
291	15.09	1.20	1.12	4.06	7.50
292	22.61	2.38	0.86	2.51	4.85
293	15.63	1.20	1.22	4.04	6.65
294	19.87	1.54	0.97	3.10	4.60
295	16.00	1.23	1.12	3.91	5.30
296	22.73	1.33	0.86	2.90	9.25
297	27.00	2.10	1.07	1.63	3.39
298	17.00	1.28	1.09	2.95	5.12
299	15.90	1.17	1.24	3.73	5.72
300	19.50	1.39	1.07	2.26	4.00
301	17.50	1.27	0.99	3.35	5.00
302	25.50	2.40	1.02	1.98	4.80
303	16.00	1.31	1.07	3.66	5.10
304	14.90	1.20	0.97	3.89	7.80
305	17.12	1.33	1.07	3.99	6.50
306	16.50	1.41	0.86	2.90	5.31

Contd.

1	*2*	*3*	*4*	*5*	*6*
307	21.00	2.11	0.76	2.13	4.42
308	15.90	1.49	1.02	2.95	5.43
309	19.80	2.15	0.81	2.84	5.74
310	18.50	1.47	1.02	2.51	5.12
311	17.11	1.32	1.07	3.73	6.32
312	19.50	2.06	0.97	2.34	3.77
313	19.10	1.51	0.81	2.51	3.52
314	19.10	2.10	0.76	2.16	3.93
315	24.40	2.37	0.86	2.67	4.20
316	18.80	1.56	0.86	3.78	5.93
317	18.00	2.01	0.86	2.74	5.55
318	26.20	3.00	0.81	2.18	3.45
319	17.66	1.37	0.97	3.28	5.55
320	18.70	2.05	0.97	3.40	4.60
321	20.00	1.50	0.97	2.51	6.00
322	19.10	1.46	0.86	3.05	4.82
323	19.40	2.12	0.94	2.72	4.48
324	23.00	2.13	0.00	2.16	3.64
325	19.20	1.52	0.86	2.59	5.15
326	19.90	1.43	0.91	2.82	4.10
327	17.70	1.54	1.07	3.10	6.20
328	16.01	1.30	1.02	3.48	7.50
329	16.50	1.21	1.07	3.53	6.15
330	18.90	1.39	0.97	2.67	5.55
331	17.28	1.30	0.91	3.25	4.70
332	17.55	1.28	0.91	3.51	4.75
333	18.04	1.37	0.97	3.89	6.45
334	20.00	2.30	0.97	2.21	3.10
335	18.00	1.40	0.91	3.43	5.00
336	15.80	1.43	0.97	3.10	5.42
337	18.10	1.50	1.07	2.44	3.61
338	16.00	1.50	1.27	3.25	5.75

Contd.

1	2	3	4	5	6
339	18.00	1.33	1.02	3.28	5.50
340	21.70	2.17	1.07	3.28	9.55
341	18.15	1.40	1.12	3.73	6.00
342	17.08	1.40	0.97	3.12	5.00
343	17.50	2.16	0.76	2.18	4.95
344	17.80	1.38	0.97	3.10	5.60
345	20.10	3.00	1.12	2.51	5.75
346	22.30	2.31	1.07	2.46	3.40
347	19.90	1.59	0.97	2.74	5.08
348	23.50	1.59	0.76	1.98	3.20
349	16.83	1.29	1.02	4.09	7.94
350	17.00	1.25	1.02	4.11	5.92
351	19.05	1.30	0.76	2.49	5.20
352	18.88	1.50	1.09	3.05	5.40
353	17.00	1.32	1.12	3.35	4.80
354	16.50	1.41	0.86	2.90	5.31
355	21.00	2.11	0.76	2.13	4.42
356	15.90	1.49	1.02	2.95	5.43
357	19.80	2.15	0.81	2.84	5.74
358	23.90	1.57	0.91	2.74	4.75
359	23.36	2.05	1.02	2.67	9.00
360	15.28	1.45	1.07	3.23	6.00
361	17.37	1.35	0.76	3.10	5.70
362	25.50	2.40	0.97	1.98	4.80
363	16.00	1.31	1.07	3.66	5.10
364	14.90	1.20	0.97	3.89	7.80
365	18.50	1.47	1.02	2.51	5.12
366	17.11	1.32	1.07	3.73	6.32
367	19.50	2.06	0.97	2.34	3.77
368	19.10	1.51	0.81	2.51	3.52
369	17.12	1.33	1.07	3.99	6.50
370	16.20	1.24	1.27	3.28	5.73

Contd.

1	2	3	4	5	6
371	17.56	1.44	1.22	3.02	5.00
372	17.00	1.47	1.12	3.30	6.69
373	18.50	1.48	1.09	3.02	6.71
374	18.50	1.47	1.02	2.51	7.24
375	17.11	1.32	1.07	3.73	6.32
376	19.50	2.06	0.97	2.34	3.77
377	19.10	1.51	0.81	2.51	3.52
378	22.29	2.10	0.91	2.87	5.50
379	19.10	2.10	0.76	2.16	3.93
380	24.40	2.37	0.86	2.67	4.20
381	18.80	1.56	0.86	3.78	5.93
382	18.00	2.01	0.86	2.74	5.55
383	20.35	2.00	1.14	2.51	4.69
384	17.50	1.33	0.99	3.07	4.33
385	25.60	2.51	1.02	2.49	5.55
386	17.60	1.24	0.97	3.05	5.08
387	18.60	2.02	1.17	2.82	4.75
388	15.60	1.19	1.12	3.73	6.60
389	14.75	1.14	1.07	4.09	7.00
390	19.11	1.58	0.86	2.84	4.90
391	16.90	2.07	1.07	3.53	5.40
392	26.20	3.00	0.81	2.18	3.45
393	17.66	1.37	0.97	3.28	5.55
394	18.70	2.05	0.97	3.40	4.60
395	20.00	1.50	0.97	2.51	6.00
396	16.00	1.28	1.07	3.63	6.10
397	21.10	2.02	1.12	2.51	4.50
398	17.80	1.36	0.91	3.35	4.60
399	19.10	2.10	0.76	2.16	3.93
400	24.40	2.37	0.86	2.67	4.20
401	18.80	1.56	0.86	3.78	5.93
402	18.00	2.01	0.86	2.74	5.55

Contd.

1	2	3	4	5	6
403	16.50	1.36	1.07	3.33	5.56
404	17.60	1.49	0.99	2.72	4.79
405	18.60	1.44	0.86	2.24	5.00
406	17.55	1.35	1.07	3.86	6.50
407	18.91	1.42	1.02	3.40	6.08
408	21.00	2.11	0.86	2.67	4.68
409	18.60	1.50	1.07	2.82	8.80
410	15.45	1.32	1.07	4.04	7.30
411	26.20	3.00	0.81	2.18	3.45
412	17.66	1.37	0.97	3.28	5.55
413	18.70	2.05	0.97	3.40	4.60
414	20.00	1.50	0.97	2.51	6.00
415	19.10	1.46	0.86	3.05	4.82
416	16.50	2.43	1.04	3.25	4.80
417	15.10	1.20	1.30	3.15	5.50
418	19.10	1.32	1.04	2.69	5.15
419	17.00	1.53	1.14	3.07	4.95
420	16.70	1.39	1.07	3.23	8.15
421	17.00	1.22	1.19	3.35	5.71
422	16.00	1.21	1.09	3.78	5.83
423	19.00	1.44	1.09	2.54	3.74
424	23.00	1.50	1.07	2.44	4.79
425	19.40	1.47	1.14	2.41	4.62
426	21.00	2.10	1.04	2.08	6.20
427	14.00	1.17	1.19	3.66	6.59
428	15.30	1.23	1.27	3.28	6.67
429	31.00	2.45	1.04	2.08	4.01
430	16.10	1.50	1.14	3.00	8.00
431	23.06	2.46	1.04	2.11	3.81
432	19.00	1.52	1.07	2.67	4.67
433	15.80	1.15	1.32	2.84	4.95
434	14.50	1.20	1.09	3.35	7.67

Contd.

1	2	3	4	5	6
435	17.50	1.30	1.07	2.16	4.87
436	17.02	2.36	1.30	3.28	4.45
437	15.80	1.24	1.24	3.51	5.93
438	18.01	1.27	1.19	2.90	5.90
439	18.00	2.20	1.07	2.29	4.95
440	17.08	1.38	1.09	3.20	4.02
441	16.20	1.32	1.14	3.23	5.06
442	23.00	1.52	1.07	1.70	3.00
443	15.03	1.14	1.30	3.40	6.08
444	15.00	1.30	1.19	2.69	6.20
445	15.90	1.17	1.24	3.73	5.72
446	19.50	1.39	1.07	2.26	4.00
447	18.80	1.48	1.04	2.44	5.73
448	17.00	2.19	1.07	2.49	6.40
449	16.10	1.24	1.09	2.54	4.50
450	16.50	1.32	1.19	3.02	5.70
451	15.60	1.40	1.14	3.30	5.95
452	24.00	2.14	1.14	2.90	5.76
453	14.20	1.18	1.22	4.78	6.78
454	20.00	1.41	0.91	2.79	5.85
455	16.80	1.27	0.91	3.48	5.68
456	19.00	2.30	0.97	2.87	6.10
457	18.80	1.41	1.22	2.95	8.54
458	18.00	1.36	0.91	2.90	6.28
459	21.00	2.14	0.86	2.95	5.82
460	19.00	1.34	0.89	3.18	5.50
461	19.20	2.05	1.07	3.43	5.08
462	15.51	1.16	1.17	3.89	5.85
463	27.41	3.08	0.76	1.88	4.58
464	16.00	1.28	1.07	3.61	4.92
465	17.10	1.32	0.86	2.69	5.10
466	17.58	1.36	0.91	3.43	5.22

Contd.

1	2	3	4	5	6
467	16.30	1.24	1.19	3.56	5.92
468	20.00	1.46	1.07	2.49	4.30
469	15.10	1.27	1.30	3.86	6.51
470	16.80	1.20	1.35	3.38	6.34
471	15.00	1.14	1.24	3.96	7.22
472	20.00	1.49	1.04	2.62	5.59
473	18.07	1.34	1.14	2.59	4.50
474	15.48	1.42	1.09	3.71	6.02
475	19.50	1.36	0.94	3.40	4.60
476	15.74	1.28	1.07	3.53	6.34
477	21.03	2.29	0.91	2.87	4.80
478	26.41	2.23	0.97	2.26	3.00
479	18.00	1.30	1.07	3.12	4.36
480	18.00	1.31	1.07	3.12	5.92
481	22.00	2.14	0.91	2.57	6.04
482	19.00	2.00	0.91	2.67	9.14
483	17.25	1.30	1.02	3.73	5.42
484	21.09	1.21	0.86	2.82	5.40
485	23.00	2.09	1.04	1.22	3.65
486	17.20	1.45	1.19	3.15	6.15
487	15.60	1.20	1.19	3.48	5.01
488	16.00	1.35	1.09	2.74	6.21
489	19.00	1.54	1.14	3.05	5.65
490	19.08	1.45	1.04	2.39	4.01
491	18.40	1.35	1.19	3.10	3.80
492	17.30	1.48	1.22	3.61	5.34
493	18.00	1.36	0.91	3.12	5.10
494	19.00	1.54	0.86	2.87	4.58
495	23.34	2.20	0.76	2.51	4.40
496	19.90	1.44	0.86	2.74	4.22
497	16.45	1.23	1.07	3.91	5.78
498	18.50	1.33	0.91	3.25	5.00

Contd.

1	*2*	*3*	*4*	*5*	*6*
499	20.40	2.04	0.97	3.78	6.15
500	16.60	1.45	1.14	3.53	6.80
501	15.00	1.17	1.35	2.41	6.20
502	17.00	1.3[illegible]	1.40	3.05	6.26
503	22.00	2.00	1.07	2.69	4.72
504	16.50	1.27	1.02	3.48	5.80
505	16.94	1.35	1.02	3.15	5.25
506	18.97	1.43	0.76	2.62	5.85
507	16.45	1.30	0.86	3.89	5.72
508	18.80	1.35	0.97	3.20	4.75
509	18.90	1.40	0.86	2.84	5.70
510	16.01	1.36	1.02	3.78	5.90
511	17.04	1.22	0.97	2.97	5.75
512	18.05	1.34	1.02	3.40	6.10
513	20.27	1.50	0.97	3.00	4.70
514	14.98	1.20	1.17	4.09	6.50
515	20.10	2.05	0.97	2.74	5.15
516	17.00	1.29	0.97	2.92	4.55
517	17.02	1.37	0.97	3.56	4.95
518	19.61	1.52	0.81	3.35	5.55
519	16.03	1.33	1.09	3.28	6.51
520	16.01	1.32	1.09	2.90	5.00
521	17.20	1.37	1.09	3.30	5.04
522	20.00	2.01	0.97	2.74	5.90
523	17.90	1.37	0.86	2.87	4.90
524	25.90	3.04	0.91	2.74	5.05
525	15.90	1.25	0.97	4.11	7.10
526	22.70	2.29	0.81	2.97	5.60
527	17.50	1.40	0.81	3.45	6.85
528	20.90	2.05	0.81	2.74	4.85
529	20.20	1.50	0.81	2.87	4.90
530	22.67	2.19	0.81	2.79	4.70

Contd.

1	2	3	4	5	6
531	17.37	1.36	1.02	2.79	9.20
532	26.60	1.46	0.81	3.18	5.95
533	17.81	1.31	0.91	3.78	6.50
534	18.70	1.33	0.81	3.96	6.80
535	19.00	2.00	0.81	2.74	6.50
536	20.00	2.05	1.09	3.30	4.37
537	17.30	1.29	1.09	3.30	4.89
538	17.50	1.28	1.09	3.02	4.98
539	16.00	1.28	1.07	3.61	4.92
540	17.10	1.32	0.86	2.69	5.10
541	17.58	1.36	0.91	3.43	5.22
542	16.30	1.24	1.19	3.56	5.92
543	16.10	1.32	1.19	3.38	5.66
544	18.30	3.04	0.81	3.23	8.40
545	15.80	1.20	1.09	3.10	4.36
546	16.80	1.27	1.09	3.15	4.14
547	15.10	1.18	1.24	3.51	6.01
548	20.00	2.31	1.07	2.18	3.70
549	16.70	1.39	1.07	3.23	8.15
550	17.00	1.22	1.19	3.35	5.71
551	16.00	1.21	1.09	3.78	5.83
552	19.00	1.44	1.09	2.54	3.74
553	21.30	2.18	1.09	2.34	5.88
554	20.00	1.46	1.07	2.49	4.30
555	15.10	1.27	1.30	3.86	6.51
556	16.80	1.20	1.35	3.38	6.34
557	15.00	1.14	1.24	3.96	7.22
558	19.28	1.51	0.97	2.84	4.73
559	17.50	2.24	1.22	3.07	4.58
560	18.90	1.45	0.97	2.26	2.97
561	16.50	1.21	0.91	2.74	5.40
562	18.40	1.40	1.14	2.67	5.29

Contd.

1	*2*	*3*	*4*	*5*	*6*
563	19.40	1.39	1.02	2.39	6.12
564	25.00	2.06	0.81	2.16	4.09
565	18.25	1.35	1.02	3.02	4.49
566	17.00	1.30	1.07	3.15	5.34
567	20.00	1.54	1.02	2.62	4.90
568	20.00	1.49	1.04	2.62	5.59
569	18.07	1.34	1.14	2.59	4.50
570	15.48	1.42	1.09	3.71	6.02
571	19.50	1.36	0.94	3.40	4.60
572	19.00	1.56	0.91	2.36	4.90
573	19.00	1.40	1.07	3.10	5.40
574	19.20	1.45	1.30	2.51	5.77
575	14.80	1.15	1.24	3.33	8.45
576	15.08	1.50	1.09	2.84	5.62
577	16.00	1.42	1.02	2.16	3.35
578	21.30	1.41	1.07	3.07	5.00
579	17.25	1.53	1.07	3.33	5.05
580	18.00	1.50	0.81	2.16	3.90
581	17.80	1.34	1.02	2.92	5.60
582	22.00	1.85	0.76	2.16	2.68
583	18.40	2.25	0.91	3.07	5.00
584	17.00	1.43	0.86	2.51	5.60
585	16.20	1.41	0.91	3.07	5.00
586	18.00	1.38	1.12	3.23	6.10
587	24.00	2.00	1.07	1.83	3.71
588	27.00	2.10	1.07	1.63	3.39
589	17.00	1.28	1.09	2.95	5.12
590	19.00	1.29	1.07	2.82	5.79
591	17.89	1.34	1.07	2.74	5.10
592	14.20	1.16	1.22	4.04	5.20
593	16.50	1.29	1.02	3.10	5.65
594	16.00	1.36	1.17	3.07	5.00

Contd.

1	*2*	*3*	*4*	*5*	*6*
595	17.00	1.36	0.97	2.57	5.85
596	17.40	1.27	1.02	2.87	5.39
597	14.00	1.20	1.17	4.01	6.90
598	19.40	1.50	0.91	3.18	6.10
599	23.60	1.35	0.91	2.41	6.49
600	17.50	1.49	1.22	3.18	6.00
601	16.00	2.00	0.91	2.67	7.00
602	16.00	1.30	1.02	2.95	6.14
603	16.90	1.44	1.14	2.49	5.40
604	15.60	1.28	1.19	2.74	5.57
605	18.00	1.48	1.09	3.18	6.08
606	16.10	1.15	1.35	3.10	6.90
607	20.50	1.35	1.07	3.71	5.03
608	15.00	1.30	1.12	3.15	6.66
609	16.50	1.35	1.12	3.51	6.51
610	19.00	1.59	1.07	2.77	5.18
611	16.10	1.38	1.07	3.25	6.51
612	16.50	1.40	1.07	3.20	6.10
613	18.00	1.55	0.91	2.67	5.65
614	18.70	1.34	1.07	2.79	5.80
615	19.00	1.51	1.07	2.67	4.73
616	19.90	1.55	0.91	2.84	4.81
617	17.00	1.48	1.07	2.95	4.20
618	15.70	1.40	1.07	3.48	6.87
619	13.50	1.26	1.22	3.35	6.66
620	16.90	1.41	1.07	3.15	5.49
621	16.20	1.25	1.24	3.05	5.83
622	16.05	1.40	1.19	3.35	5.50
623	17.03	1.31	1.19	3.18	5.44
624	15.03	1.30	1.09	3.56	6.92
625	15.80	1.54	1.04	2.87	6.02
626	15.90	1.50	1.12	2.21	4.32
627	15.80	1.40	1.30	3.78	6.75
628	18.60	1.35	1.14	2.82	5.13

APPENDIX-3

PECET-PHYSICAL EFFICIENCY TEST STANDARD SCORES (QUALIFIED MEN CANDIDATES)

S.No.	100M	800M	High	Long	Shot	Criterion
1	60	0	20	27	43	150
2	61	0	20	25	44	150
3	51	0	30	31	38	150
4	51	0	20	50	29	150
5	48	0	30	30	42	150
6	36	18	25	27	44	150
7	52	0	20	28	50	150
8	0	100	0	17	34	151
9	51	0	30	30	40	151
10	44	32	15	22	38	151
11	42	0	30	34	45	151
12	58	0	30	21	42	151
13	64	0	15	34	39	152
14	49	0	30	33	40	152
15	51	0	30	22	49	152
16	53	18	25	21	35	152
17	54	0	20	23	45	152
18	51	0	38	25	38	152

Contd.

1	2	3	4	5	6	7
19	55	0	38	23	36	152
20	47	0	20	39	47	153
21	43	0	38	33	39	153
22	52	0	50	21	30	153
23	52	0	30	28	43	153
24	54	18	25	23	33	153
25	61	0	25	27	40	153
26	54	0	38	22	39	153
27	55	0	20	36	42	153
28	48	18	20	34	34	154
29	46	0	25	34	49	154
30	40	30	25	25	34	154
31	51	0	10	50	44	155
32	58	0	10	38	49	155
33	58	0	20	38	39	155
34	42	0	50	24	39	155
35	54	0	25	25	51	155
36	48	0	55	18	35	156
37	46	22	30	27	31	156
38	54	0	38	25	39	156
39	53	0	38	22	43	156
40	60	0	20	39	37	156
41	68	0	15	28	45	156
42	53	0	15	45	43	156
43	48	10	25	23	50	156
44	50	0	30	38	39	157
45	50	0	20	51	36	157
46	42	18	57	0	40	157
47	52	43	0	27	35	157
48	58	0	30	30	39	157
49	54	0	38	28	38	158

Contd.

1	*2*	*3*	*4*	*5*	*6*	*7*
50	54	0	25	35	44	158
51	23	100	0	0	35	158
52	54	0	20	40	45	159
53	52	0	30	40	37	159
54	54	0	50	18	37	159
55	54	0	38	25	42	150
56	0	100	10	15	34	159
57	58	0	30	30	41	159
58	51	0	15	50	44	160
59	46	0	38	40	36	160
60	58	0	10	40	52	160
61	38	28	30	31	34	161
62	0	100	25	0	36	161
63	58	0	33	34	36	161
64	52	0	20	50	39	161
65	61	0	25	30	45	161
66	54	0	30	31	47	162
67	49	25	30	22	36	162
68	52	28	25	22	35	162
69	51	18	15	32	46	162
70	54	13	25	30	40	162
71	58	0	10	41	53	162
72	28	0	67	22	45	162
73	43	42	15	16	47	163
74	64	0	38	23	38	163
75	49	0	50	20	44	163
76	54	0	10	46	53	163
77	49	20	20	33	41	163
78	44	22	30	28	39	163
79	46	0	60	17	40	163
80	48	0	50	25	40	163
81	44	32	30	22	36	164

Contd.

1	*2*	*3*	*4*	*5*	*6*	*7*
82	51	0	38	24	51	164
83	52	0	38	26	48	164
84	51	0	20	40	53	164
85	51	15	30	27	41	164
86	58	0	38	24	44	164
87	52	0	38	26	48	164
88	40	42	25	22	35	164
89	54	10	30	33	37	164
90	51	0	30	47	36	164
91	58	0	38	32	36	164
92	45	0	15	58	47	165
93	46	0	30	42	47	165
94	45	13	38	32	37	165
95	54	0	38	38	35	165
96	67	0	20	35	43	165
97	50	23	25	27	41	166
98	58	0	38	27	43	166
99	58	0	30	38	41	167
100	44	0	0	23	100	167
101	51	0	38	38	40	167
102	45	37	15	32	38	167
103	54	10	25	33	45	167
104	48	0	50	23	46	167
105	58	0	33	36	40	167
106	50	0	55	23	39	167
107	0	100	15	10	43	168
108	63	0	38	23	44	168
109	39	0	55	22	52	168
110	49	0	50	32	37	168
111	44	15	38	34	37	168
112	51	0	30	45	43	169
113	67	0	20	42	40	169

Contd.

1	*2*	*3*	*4*	*5*	*6*	*7*
114	58	0	25	40	46	169
115	51	32	20	28	38	169
116	64	0	30	31	44	169
117	53	0	20	43	53	169
118	65	0	25	43	36	169
119	60	18	10	43	38	169
120	54	0	38	34	43	169
121	43	0	65	21	40	169
122	58	0	30	36	46	170
123	55	0	30	45	40	170
124	53	20	38	22	37	170
125	58	0	30	34	48	170
126	42	13	50	26	39	170
127	58	0	38	30	44	170
128	43	0	67	22	39	171
129	52	10	33	36	40	171
130	44	48	25	21	33	171
131	58	0	60	13	40	171
132	58	0	33	26	54	171
133	58	0	10	51	52	171
134	44	0	30	52	45	171
135	54	0	25	40	52	171
136	67	0	25	41	39	172
137	50	0	25	52	45	172
138	52	13	38	28	41	172
139	46	0	38	38	50	172
140	49	0	15	59	49	172
141	53	15	30	38	37	173
142	48	0	50	23	52	173
143	48	0	67	23	35	173
144	58	0	30	38	47	173
145	58	0	38	34	43	173

Contd.

1	2	3	4	5	6	7
146	51	0	38	40	44	173
147	51	10	20	49	43	173
148	43	40	25	20	46	174
149	48	41	25	20	40	174
150	51	0	55	24	44	174
151	54	20	20	36	44	174
152	52	0	50	23	50	175
153	54	0	30	36	55	175
154	63	23	15	30	44	175
155	53	0	38	35	49	175
156	61	22	15	38	40	176
157	46	0	38	53	39	176
158	51	43	30	22	30	176
159	58	0	30	34	54	176
160	42	35	20	41	38	176
161	55	28	30	35	35	176
162	44	100	0	0	32	176
163	52	0	30	53	41	176
164	53	0	50	30	43	176
165	54	32	30	26	35	177
166	54	0	50	34	39	177
167	47	15	33	36	46	177
168	70	10	30	25	42	177
169	45	42	33	23	35	178
170	51	0	50	28	49	178
171	54	18	30	41	35	178
172	65	0	38	36	39	178
173	53	25	20	42	38	178
174	45	22	50	25	36	178
175	44	0	67	35	32	178
176	64	0	38	23	53	178
177	83	0	20	38	38	179

Contd.

1	*2*	*3*	*4*	*5*	*6*	*7*
178	51	10	30	47	41	179
179	28	100	0	16	35	179
180	68	33	20	20	38	179
181	58	0	50	25	46	179
182	51	0	50	43	35	179
183	49	41	20	34	36	180
184	50	0	50	39	41	180
185	58	38	25	34	25	180
186	40	37	33	28	42	180
187	60	37	10	31	42	180
188	53	0	50	34	43	180
189	70	0	38	31	42	181
190	51	33	15	40	42	181
191	50	0	67	23	42	182
192	65	41	10	22	44	182
193	43	18	38	39	44	182
194	46	40	30	19	48	183
195	52	40	25	28	38	183
196	54	39	30	21	39	183
197	55	0	38	44	46	183
198	64	0	33	36	50	183
199	49	10	50	40	34	183
200	55	39	10	36	43	183
201	48	0	67	24	44	183
202	54	0	55	33	42	184
203	50	0	67	22	45	184
204	46	0	65	32	41	184
205	38	100	0	18	28	184
206	52	20	25	41	46	184
207	51	100	0	0	33	184
208	52	15	50	28	39	184
209	52	32	25	32	43	184

Contd.

1	*2*	*3*	*4*	*5*	*6*	*7*
210	65	22	25	33	39	184
211	58	0	67	19	40	184
212	68	15	25	24	53	185
213	60	20	30	39	36	185
214	51	0	38	46	50	185
215	44	20	33	47	41	185
216	54	18	25	35	53	185
217	58	0	38	48	41	185
218	45	0	55	50	36	186
219	73	0	50	28	35	186
220	65	13	30	33	45	186
221	51	0	38	50	47	186
222	51	30	30	40	35	186
223	50	0	67	28	41	186
224	55	0	50	38	44	187
225	52	15	67	18	35	187
226	54	0	55	40	38	187
227	58	32	20	40	37	187
228	51	0	38	48	50	187
229	51	32	30	32	42	187
230	54	0	67	23	44	188
231	51	0	55	40	43	189
232	64	0	30	44	51	189
233	65	0	50	33	41	189
234	55	0	67	32	35	189
235	54	0	55	38	42	189
236	68	10	20	44	47	189
237	53	23	30	42	41	189
238	50	23	50	30	36	189
239	64	0	38	42	46	190
240	54	30	30	24	52	190
241	54	10	38	47	41	190

Contd.

1	*2*	*3*	*4*	*5*	*6*	*7*
242	52	0	60	40	38	190
243	67	35	0	47	42	191
244	52	0	67	27	45	191
245	53	0	67	23	48	191
246	58	0	50	40	43	191
247	60	33	30	28	41	192
248	51	100	15	26	0	192
249	58	0	67	22	45	192
250	49	32	25	50	36	192
251	54	32	38	34	34	193
252	60	10	38	40	45	193
253	65	10	38	42	38	193
254	51	0	52	46	44	193
255	50	42	38	27	36	193
256	58	0	55	33	47	193
257	60	28	30	32	43	193
258	54	18	38	40	43	194
259	54	44	25	36	35	194
260	61	41	10	41	41	194
261	51	0	50	44	49	194
262	49	28	30	45	42	194
263	49	23	30	51	41	194
264	58	28	30	31	47	195
265	52	0	67	36	40	195
266	70	39	20	28	38	195
267	58	0	50	40	47	195
268	61	35	30	31	38	195
269	48	0	67	32	48	195
270	60	37	33	28	37	195
271	68	23	25	34	45	195
272	61	20	20	46	48	195
273	54	33	30	31	47	196

Contd.

1	2	3	4	5	6	7
274	52	0	55	36	53	196
275	51	0	67	34	44	196
276	75	0	50	27	44	196
277	54	0	38	53	51	196
278	23	0	67	56	50	197
279	54	0	50	53	40	197
280	55	0	67	30	45	197
281	54	10	38	45	50	198
282	64	0	38	50	46	198
283	53	0	55	48	42	198
284	65	28	30	35	40	198
285	48	0	38	58	54	198
286	58	15	38	46	41	198
287	61	0	55	38	44	198
288	60	20	38	40	40	198
289	67	38	25	28	40	199
290	85	13	30	23	48	199
291	39	100	0	18	42	199
292	50	40	30	36	43	199
293	55	0	55	41	48	199
294	58	0	50	48	43	199
295	64	40	15	31	49	200
296	61	0	38	55	46	200
297	72	22	33	32	41	200
298	63	15	33	44	45	200
299	58	28	30	34	50	200
300	54	0	50	48	48	217
301	54	0	65	32	50	201
302	53	0	67	31	50	201
303	61	0	38	45	57	201
304	60	0	50	43	48	201
305	65	0	67	24	46	202

Contd.

1	2	3	4	5	6	7
306	64	0	65	23	50	202
307	49	0	67	41	45	202
308	53	38	30	42	39	202
309	55	35	33	35	44	202
310	68	0	55	38	41	202
311	63	0	55	50	35	203
312	49	41	30	46	37	203
313	52	22	55	28	46	203
314	48	22	67	22	45	204
315	61	0	65	35	43	204
316	54	0	60	48	42	204
317	73	0	50	36	45	204
318	61	25	38	40	41	205
319	72	0	67	18	48	205
320	60	0	65	33	47	205
321	61	0	55	40	49	205
322	51	0	60	50	44	205
323	38	100	0	22	45	205
324	45	28	55	31	46	205
325	61	33	30	45	36	205
326	60	0	50	47	48	205
327	51	35	50	23	47	206
328	54	35	20	54	43	206
329	39	13	60	50	44	206
330	63	0	60	32	51	206
331	61	13	38	53	42	207
332	54	41	20	51	41	207
333	54	32	38	44	39	207
334	58	0	67	50	33	208
335	30	100	20	12	45	208
336	64	30	30	44	40	208

Contd.

1	*2*	*3*	*4*	*5*	*6*	*7*
337	55	30	30	48	45	208
338	52	15	65	42	34	208
339	61	0	50	61	37	209
340	33	100	15	25	36	209
341	61	0	67	36	45	209
342	54	23	38	50	44	209
343	68	0	65	25	52	210
344	61	10	55	38	46	210
345	54	22	38	46	50	210
346	49	23	67	23	48	210
347	49	100	0	20	41	210
348	54	32	55	23	46	210
349	78	60	10	23	40	211
350	52	47	38	36	38	211
351	52	25	50	42	42	211
352	70	10	38	58	35	211
353	54	22	67	36	32	211
354	58	20	38	55	41	212
355	65	0	55	45	47	212
356	47	20	67	38	40	212
357	52	42	30	47	41	212
358	55	0	67	38	52	212
359	58	51	25	38	40	212
360	65	32	30	45	40	212
361	51	15	60	41	45	212
362	68	43	20	46	35	212
363	54	32	50	35	41	212
364	52	0	67	50	44	213
365	55	51	38	24	45	213
366	61	10	55	42	45	213
367	64	0	67	34	48	213

Contd.

1	*2*	*3*	*4*	*5*	*6*	*7*
368	54	0	67	47	45	213
369	61	47	33	34	38	213
370	50	13	55	50	45	213
371	53	30	50	41	40	214
372	64	0	60	42	48	214
373	68	0	60	41	45	214
374	54	40	33	50	38	215
375	58	0	67	43	47	215
376	55	33	33	48	46	215
377	53	47	33	38	44	215
378	48	30	50	41	46	215
379	64	28	38	41	44	215
380	65	41	15	46	48	215
381	64	0	50	44	57	215
382	72	0	50	45	48	215
383	52	55	33	40	35	215
384	52	0	67	48	48	215
385	60	37	38	39	41	215
386	60	45	38	27	45	215
387	68	0	60	33	54	215
388	53	15	50	50	47	215
389	58	37	50	27	43	215
390	53	23	67	33	40	216
391	54	25	67	31	39	216
392	70	0	50	54	42	216
393	70	23	60	25	38	216
394	63	23	38	48	44	216
395	67	43	20	42	44	216
396	54	20	67	41	34	216
397	51	0	60	47	58	216
398	54	22	60	35	45	216
399	58	41	30	41	46	216

Contd.

1	*2*	*3*	*4*	*5*	*6*	*7*
400	61	0	60	45	50	216
401	63	18	38	53	45	217
402	70	0	50	50	47	217
403	51	37	20	60	49	217
404	68	42	10	51	46	217
405	63	10	50	53	41	217
406	64	0	67	42	44	218
407	67	0	55	46	50	218
408	70	40	15	51	42	218
409	60	30	30	59	39	218
410	61	0	60	42	55	218
411	54	40	50	35	39	218
412	52	49	30	40	47	218
413	55	18	67	30	48	219
414	72	0	67	33	47	219
415	43	100	10	21	45	219
416	52	0	55	59	53	219
417	67	38	15	53	46	219
418	58	42	38	41	40	219
419	63	41	33	30	52	220
420	61	0	75	38	46	220
421	51	45	30	54	40	220
422	61	37	30	53	39	220
423	43	47	25	47	58	220
424	70	0	60	35	55	220
425	52	0	65	60	43	220
426	73	35	38	34	40	220
427	75	33	30	32	50	220
428	67	39	33	36	45	220
429	64	23	50	49	34	221
430	75	0	60	44	42	221
431	51	43	38	50	39	221

Contd.

1	*2*	*3*	*4*	*5*	*6*	*7*
432	54	0	67	50	50	222
433	54	88	25	16	39	222
434	51	15	60	50	46	222
435	55	38	50	36	43	222
436	73	42	30	28	49	222
437	65	52	38	28	39	222
438	60	28	50	46	38	222
439	77	32	30	40	43	222
440	60	0	60	53	49	223
441	61	32	50	34	46	223
442	54	48	30	51	40	223
443	67	47	30	32	47	223
444	64	45	33	45	36	224
445	49	85	33	22	35	225
446	53	40	67	30	35	225
447	72	54	20	36	43	225
448	65	53	25	43	39	225
449	64	51	30	34	46	225
450	55	15	67	41	47	241
451	67	28	38	46	46	225
452	55	30	67	32	41	225
453	50	88	25	25	37	225
454	54	36	55	43	37	225
455	67	40	33	36	49	225
456	54	33	55	38	46	226
457	67	39	30	45	45	226
458	73	43	38	32	40	226
459	60	18	38	62	48	226
460	68	40	55	17	46	226
461	58	46	38	41	44	227
462	70	41	38	31	47	227
463	70	0	50	61	46	227

Contd.

1	*2*	*3*	*4*	*5*	*6*	*7*
464	73	37	33	43	41	227
465	73	18	50	41	45	227
466	54	35	52	36	50	227
467	68	39	33	41	47	228
468	73	0	67	41	47	228
469	73	40	30	36	49	228
470	51	25	67	38	47	228
471	54	45	50	38	41	228
472	54	32	67	30	45	228
473	72	0	67	45	45	229
474	65	18	60	36	50	229
475	73	46	20	50	40	229
476	54	25	67	38	45	229
477	54	35	50	44	46	229
478	64	0	67	53	45	229
479	55	25	55	52	42	229
480	65	41	20	50	54	230
481	54	35	67	36	38	230
482	58	18	38	61	55	230
483	75	61	15	42	37	230
484	65	10	50	56	49	230
485	54	43	50	44	39	230
486	55	36	50	51	39	231
487	64	0	65	46	56	231
488	70	36	38	41	46	231
489	65	37	50	39	40	231
490	58	85	25	28	35	231
491	54	36	67	34	40	231
492	58	37	55	40	42	232
493	52	89	25	23	43	232
494	64	10	60	48	50	232
495	65	25	38	64	40	232

Contd.

1	*2*	*3*	*4*	*5*	*6*	*7*
496	54	37	57	38	46	232
497	53	20	55	51	54	232
498	67	37	38	44	47	233
499	63	0	50	64	56	233
500	67	33	38	58	37	233
501	73	0	60	58	42	233
502	63	53	33	46	39	234
503	50	33	67	45	39	234
504	73	39	10	64	48	234
505	61	0	65	61	47	234
506	63	15	65	52	39	234
507	64	40	55	28	47	234
508	65	15	65	47	42	234
509	70	42	30	45	47	234
510	73	30	38	52	41	234
511	77	0	67	39	51	234
512	50	23	72	43	47	235
513	64	20	50	53	48	235
514	51	49	67	23	45	235
515	52	32	55	38	38	235
516	73	0	60	58	44	235
517	61	40	55	40	40	236
518	39	100	38	20	39	236
519	68	36	50	36	46	236
520	64	33	60	38	41	236
521	65	50	30	43	48	236
522	67	18	67	45	39	236
523	70	0	65	53	48	236
524	68	36	38	56	38	236
525	77	0	67	50	42	236
526	51	100	25	24	36	236
527	60	43	55	36	43	237

Contd.

1	2	3	4	5	6	7
528	54	0	100	44	39	237
529	70	25	50	51	41	237
530	61	39	57	41	39	237
531	64	0	70	58	46	238
532	63	50	15	61	49	238
533	70	30	55	40	43	238
534	75	38	20	52	53	238
535	64	40	38	50	46	238
536	48	20	65	64	41	238
537	75	46	33	49	35	238
538	68	32	50	46	43	239
539	60	61	30	46	42	239
540	64	18	67	50	40	239
541	60	25	60	48	46	239
542	52	32	67	45	43	239
543	54	33	60	45	47	239
544	51	35	50	38	45	239
545	70	53	30	46	41	240
546	65	42	67	24	42	240
547	72	23	38	62	45	240
548	64	38	38	55	45	240
549	77	20	67	40	37	241
550	68	0	67	40	66	241
551	63	36	60	38	44	242
552	55	55	38	54	40	242
553	53	35	67	43	44	242
554	53	50	67	31	41	242
555	63	45	50	50	34	242
556	67	32	43	51	49	242
557	60	39	50	52	41	242
558	72	35	55	36	44	242
559	63	28	50	47	54	242

Contd.

1	2	3	4	5	6	7
560	44	100	30	24	44	243
561	72	33	67	36	35	243
562	60	39	55	53	36	243
563	53	35	67	39	49	243
564	60	33	55	56	39	243
565	50	48	67	35	43	243
566	80	0	60	56	47	243
567	55	39	55	46	48	243
568	49	38	60	48	48	243
569	70	30	50	50	43	244
570	70	23	50	54	47	244
571	52	49	67	31	45	244
572	65	25	65	47	42	244
573	95	0	55	47	47	244
574	73	42	33	48	48	244
575	70	42	55	42	35	245
576	77	51	0	71	46	245
577	67	52	38	48	40	245
578	53	100	15	36	41	245
579	72	18	65	45	45	246
580	61	43	38	45	59	246
581	75	0	67	64	40	246
582	61	25	65	52	43	246
583	63	47	50	46	40	246
584	70	39	50	33	54	246
585	83	42	38	39	44	246
586	58	36	67	39	46	247
587	77	0	67	53	50	247
588	68	47	55	44	33	247
589	61	39	67	34	46	247
590	65	48	33	53	48	247
591	70	23	65	42	47	247

Contd.

1	*2*	*3*	*4*	*5*	*6*	*7*
592	63	28	60	43	53	248
593	58	22	67	47	54	248
594	83	44	25	48	48	248
595	67	15	60	59	47	249
596	67	52	55	36	39	250
597	46	100	38	23	43	250
598	78	48	33	53	38	250
599	54	41	50	58	47	251
600	64	41	38	65	43	271
601	55	39	67	47	43	251
602	63	44	60	41	43	251
603	68	33	50	50	50	251
604	60	41	55	48	47	251
605	78	56	38	43	37	252
606	67	23	65	57	40	252
607	54	51	65	41	41	252
608	88	0	60	56	49	253
609	72	33	60	47	41	253
610	61	25	60	53	54	253
611	67	0	70	70	46	253
612	68	100	20	23	42	253
613	68	25	55	59	46	253
614	61	46	50	52	45	254
615	75	0	67	62	51	255
616	70	40	60	40	45	255
617	75	10	55	58	57	255
618	67	30	65	51	42	255
619	60	38	67	48	43	256
620	67	53	67	23	46	256
621	68	49	38	53	48	256
622	61	20	70	60	45	256
623	67	45	55	47	42	256

Contd.

1	2	3	4	5	6	7
624	73	42	38	61	43	257
625	54	39	70	52	42	257
626	64	41	67	45	40	257
627	65	33	65	46	48	257
628	61	40	50	67	39	257
629	61	47	50	54	46	258
630	60	43	60	45	50	258
631	61	23	60	61	54	259
632	60	25	60	66	48	259
633	58	48	67	46	40	259
634	70	44	50	51	44	259
635	48	85	67	23	36	259
636	73	32	67	41	46	259
637	72	48	52	40	47	259
638	70	47	67	30	46	260
639	54	49	67	44	46	260
640	73	56	33	48	50	260
641	65	56	50	50	39	260
642	73	45	38	50	54	260
643	64	38	55	59	44	260
644	58	89	33	36	44	260
645	67	30	50	69	44	260
646	73	35	65	46	41	260
647	75	50	50	46	40	261
648	60	50	67	44	40	261
649	78	52	38	50	43	261
650	65	0	75	73	48	261
651	77	33	55	47	49	261
652	67	38	67	50	39	261
653	54	100	20	48	40	262
654	61	43	50	58	50	262
655	68	55	55	41	43	262

Contd.

1	2	3	4	5	6	7
656	54	42	65	51	50	262
657	78	61	38	44	41	262
658	77	46	50	48	41	262
659	77	0	65	71	49	262
660	65	62	67	32	37	263
661	65	39	67	50	42	263
662	63	32	50	75	43	263
663	75	38	67	39	44	263
664	54	42	67	43	57	263
665	70	40	50	52	51	263
666	65	51	67	45	35	263
667	55	46	67	46	50	264
668	73	56	55	38	42	264
669	70	40	60	54	40	264
670	68	53	38	61	45	265
671	63	40	60	56	46	265
672	85	20	60	55	45	265
673	61	42	55	59	48	265
674	73	32	67	48	45	265
675	52	51	67	54	42	266
676	63	44	50	61	48	266
677	60	45	67	51	43	266
678	68	36	55	58	49	266
679	100	0	50	66	50	266
680	77	23	65	52	49	266
681	67	30	50	67	53	267
682	61	40	55	67	44	267
683	85	20	65	52	45	267
684	65	32	67	53	50	267
685	80	40	65	45	37	267
686	75	38	50	58	47	268
687	63	35	67	53	50	268

Contd.

1	*2*	*3*	*4*	*5*	*6*	*7*
688	61	50	65	51	41	268
689	75	48	55	52	38	268
690	80	46	55	36	51	268
691	64	44	67	43	51	269
692	67	55	67	36	45	270
693	70	40	55	59	46	270
694	75	20	65	53	58	271
695	65	43	67	58	38	271
696	77	36	60	51	47	271
697	67	58	65	32	49	271
698	64	44	65	56	42	271
699	73	44	67	47	40	271
700	67	50	67	45	42	271
701	68	50	55	50	48	272
702	72	41	67	44	48	272
703	58	41	67	56	50	273
704	67	49	70	40	47	273
705	61	57	67	50	38	273
706	65	43	67	53	45	273
707	100	46	50	41	36	273
708	73	0	70	76	54	273
709	67	42	60	62	42	273
710	58	43	67	49	56	274
711	63	42	65	58	46	274
712	75	44	57	49	49	275
713	72	36	67	41	59	276
714	73	41	50	67	45	276
715	77	45	50	54	50	276
716	75	54	67	45	35	276
717	72	39	60	64	41	276
718	65	65	67	39	40	277
719	78	65	50	46	38	277

Contd.

1	2	3	4	5	6	7
720	70	54	67	45	41	277
721	88	43	25	64	57	278
722	64	61	55	56	42	278
723	72	45	67	52	42	278
724	75	33	67	54	49	278
725	73	32	67	53	53	279
726	77	60	55	52	35	279
727	65	53	67	45	49	279
728	100	47	30	56	46	279
729	80	25	67	59	48	280
730	67	48	60	59	46	281
731	52	89	67	28	45	282
732	73	37	65	51	56	282
733	75	42	65	61	39	282
734	67	30	67	39	59	283
735	77	49	43	62	52	283
736	78	55	38	69	43	284
737	85	43	67	44	45	284
738	77	51	55	54	47	284
739	68	60	55	59	42	284
740	64	49	67	58	46	284
741	46	100	50	40	48	284
742	75	48	67	49	45	285
743	65	49	67	53	51	285
744	73	57	60	59	36	285
745	78	47	67	53	40	285
746	68	53	67	49	48	285
747	72	53	67	50	43	286
748	68	42	65	64	47	286
749	72	47	67	53	47	286
750	68	47	65	57	49	386
751	83	48	55	51	49	286

Contd.

1	*2*	*3*	*4*	*5*	*6*	*7*
752	73	53	65	52	43	286
753	88	38	65	52	44	287
754	78	46	70	53	40	287
755	70	49	55	68	45	287
756	75	59	55	56	42	287
757	70	48	67	58	45	288
758	64	49	70	59	46	288
759	78	28	70	67	45	288
760	65	55	67	53	48	288
761	77	85	33	48	45	288
762	85	46	67	50	40	288
763	83	53	50	59	44	289
764	75	47	65	58	44	289
765	70	66	62	40	51	289
766	73	53	67	63	33	289
767	70	49	60	61	50	290
768	67	58	50	66	50	291
769	63	45	65	69	49	291
770	73	59	60	56	43	291
771	100	36	55	52	49	292
772	85	44	67	56	40	292
773	75	48	67	55	48	293
774	65	37	50	58	83	293
775	85	50	67	52	39	293
776	83	44	67	56	44	294
777	83	44	60	58	50	295
778	83	47	60	62	43	295
779	73	66	55	58	44	296
780	70	44	60	75	47	296
781	80	45	67	64	40	296
782	85	40	65	53	54	297
783	80	56	65	51	45	297
784	80	46	65	65	41	297

Contd.

1	*2*	*3*	*4*	*5*	*6*	*7*
785	51	68	60	61	57	297
786	77	47	67	60	47	298
787	67	70	65	51	46	299
788	77	46	72	64	40	299
789	75	33	67	64	60	299
790	77	54	67	53	48	299
791	85	43	55	66	51	300
792	77	42	67	62	52	300
793	83	30	70	71	47	301
794	67	50	77	59	49	302
795	80	40	70	63	49	302
796	90	50	50	67	46	303
797	78	51	67	59	48	303
798	73	54	77	56	44	304
799	64	89	67	41	43	304
800	77	47	65	67	48	304
801	100	44	55	61	44	304
802	78	57	55	71	43	304
803	75	59	67	56	49	306
804	73	53	67	64	50	307
805	83	42	70	70	43	308
806	61	62	67	67	52	309
807	49	77	67	55	62	310
808	95	49	67	51	49	311
809	85	32	82	67	46	312
810	75	56	67	61	53	312
811	100	30	65	62	56	313
812	100	46	60	55	52	313
813	77	50	67	70	49	313
814	95	53	67	57	43	315
815	100	37	67	61	50	315
816	77	46	67	77	48	315
817	67	43	80	80	46	316

Contd.

1	2	3	4	5	6	7
818	83	60	67	67	40	317
819	100	100	30	35	53	318
820	78	49	67	67	57	318
821	77	68	65	58	50	318
822	85	64	65	65	39	318
823	67	100	67	44	40	318
824	88	61	55	73	42	319
825	95	28	75	72	49	319
826	78	60	75	67	41	321
827	88	46	70	69	48	321
828	63	49	100	58	52	322
829	77	73	72	47	55	324
830	75	55	65	75	55	325
831	100	51	55	76	45	327
832	100	58	50	82	38	328
833	83	67	67	67	44	328
834	95	54	65	51	65	330
835	88	59	72	71	45	335
836	80	77	67	63	49	336
837	100	41	67	72	56	336
838	73	89	67	64	43	336
839	100	70	50	78	39	337
840	100	65	67	61	46	339
841	100	39	70	70	61	340
842	100	41	70	77	52	340
843	88	52	75	70	56	341
844	77	62	70	75	59	343
845	80	43	100	67	53	343
846	77	89	67	58	56	347
847	80	72	67	69	69	357
848	85	89	72	65	50	361
849	100	90	67	64	50	371
850	100	73	67	81	55	376
851	100	95	72	70	49	

APPENDIX-4

PECET-PHYSICAL EFFICIENCY TEST STANDARD SCORES (QUALIFIED WOMEN CANDIDATES)

S.No.	*100M*	*800M*	*High*	*Long*	*Shot*	*Criterion*
1	0	100	0	25	30	155
2	18	85	0	24	29	156
3	0	100	0	24	32	156
4	48	0	55	19	37	159
5	48	0	55	19	37	159
6	0	100	10	19	31	160
7	0	100	10	19	31	160
8	0	88	30	16	30	164
9	15	100	0	20	30	165
10	18	90	0	28	29	165
11	15	100	0	20	30	165
12	18	90	0	28	29	165
13	15	100	0	20	30	165
14	0	100	15	24	29	168
15	52	0	52	36	29	169
16	0	88	30	23	28	169
17	0	88	30	23	28	169
18	52	0	52	36	29	169

Contd.

1	2	3	4	5	6	7
19	43	0	70	30	27	170
20	20	100	0	24	27	171
21	0	88	55	0	28	171
22	0	95	30	11	37	173
23	0	90	15	34	34	173
24	0	83	38	23	30	174
25	18	100	15	20	22	175
26	0	100	55	0	20	175
27	18	100	15	20	22	175
28	18	100	15	20	22	175
29	13	88	30	13	31	175
30	18	100	15	20	22	175
31	30	100	0	15	30	175
32	0	100	55	0	20	175
33	30	100	0	15	30	175
34	13	88	30	13	31	175
35	30	100	0	15	30	175
36	0	100	0	24	51	175
37	0	95	30	24	29	178
38	0	83	55	15	25	178
39	0	83	55	15	25	178
40	0	83	55	15	25	178
41	0	83	55	15	25	178
42	0	83	55	15	25	178
43	0	83	55	15	25	178
44	0	83	55	15	25	178
45	0	100	30	24	25	179
46	0	100	30	24	25	179
47	39	88	0	24	29	180
48	23	100	0	24	33	180
49	0	100	38	16	28	182
50	0	95	52	10	25	182

Contd.

1	*2*	*3*	*4*	*5*	*6*	*7*
51	0	95	52	10	25	182
52	49	0	55	46	32	182
53	35	100	0	21	27	183
54	35	100	0	21	27	183
55	20	100	0	34	32	186
56	20	90	30	17	29	186
57	0	100	30	23	34	187
58	0	100	15	40	32	187
59	0	83	52	21	32	188
60	38	100	15	11	24	188
61	0	83	52	21	32	188
62	46	0	77	38	27	188
63	46	0	77	38	27	188
64	10	83	50	10	35	188
65	0	83	52	21	32	188
66	23	100	10	21	34	188
67	0	100	38	23	28	189
68	42	88	15	10	34	189
69	23	95	38	15	19	190
70	0	90	55	19	26	190
71	0	90	55	19	26	190
72	0	90	55	19	26	190
73	0	90	55	19	26	190
74	0	90	33	41	28	192
75	0	90	33	41	28	192
76	0	85	62	11	34	192
77	0	100	38	20	35	193
78	0	100	38	20	35	193
79	0	100	38	20	35	193
80	46	100	0	17	31	194
81	46	100	0	17	31	194
82	47	100	0	18	30	195

Contd.

1	*2*	*3*	*4*	*5*	*6*	*7*
83	47	100	0	18	30	195
84	42	88	15	17	34	196
85	23	83	38	21	32	197
86	23	83	38	21	32	197
87	0	100	38	31	28	197
88	23	83	38	21	32	197
89	10	88	62	11	28	199
90	10	88	62	11	28	199
91	0	100	50	21	29	200
92	48	100	0	20	33	201
93	0	100	55	18	28	201
94	0	100	55	18	28	201
95	0	100	55	18	28	201
96	25	90	0	53	34	202
97	25	90	0	53	34	202
98	25	90	0	53	34	202
99	13	100	38	24	28	203
100	20	100	52	10	24	206
101	52	100	0	24	31	207
102	52	100	0	24	31	207
103	52	100	0	24	31	207
104	10	100	30	34	35	209
105	20	83	55	23	30	211
106	44	95	10	31	33	213
107	25	85	52	18	33	213
108	44	95	10	31	33	213
109	25	85	52	18	33	213
110	0	95	38	48	33	214
111	0	100	55	30	30	215
112	42	83	43	19	28	215
113	42	83	43	19	28	215
114	20	83	55	24	33	215

Contd.

1	*2*	*3*	*4*	*5*	*6*	*7*
115	42	83	43	19	28	215
116	33	95	33	31	24	216
117	33	95	33	31	24	216
118	37	88	33	24	34	216
119	33	95	33	31	24	216
120	37	88	33	24	34	216
121	38	95	30	21	33	217
122	32	88	50	20	27	217
123	38	90	30	24	36	218
124	18	100	52	18	30	218
125	18	100	52	18	30	218
126	32	88	50	20	30	220
127	20	100	57	20	23	220
128	38	90	30	32	30	220
129	20	100	57	20	23	220
130	20	100	57	20	23	220
131	32	88	50	20	30	220
132	20	100	57	20	23	220
133	20	100	57	20	23	220
134	25	95	38	35	28	221
135	48	83	38	25	27	221
136	20	100	55	14	33	222
137	20	100	55	21	28	224
138	20	100	55	21	28	224
139	20	100	55	21	28	224
140	38	90	38	23	37	226
141	40	85	38	31	33	227
142	32	100	30	36	30	228
143	40	90	30	40	28	228
144	20	100	62	23	24	229
145	42	85	30	45	28	230
146	48	90	38	20	34	230

Contd.

1	2	3	4	5	6	7
147	35	95	50	23	27	230
148	42	85	30	45	28	230
149	0	95	55	51	30	231
150	32	88	50	20	41	231
151	20	85	72	24	32	233
152	37	100	55	18	23	233
153	20	85	72	24	32	233
154	37	100	55	18	23	233
155	48	83	38	41	24	234
156	25	100	38	25	47	235
157	32	85	57	23	38	235
158	42	90	30	42	31	235
159	32	85	57	23	38	235
160	48	88	50	21	28	235
161	42	90	30	42	31	235
162	41	88	38	38	32	237
163	64	85	33	23	32	237
164	41	88	38	38	32	237
165	28	100	62	20	27	237
166	43	85	57	23	29	237
167	64	85	33	23	32	237
168	43	85	57	23	29	237
169	64	85	33	23	32	237
170	28	100	62	20	27	237
171	44	88	50	24	31	237
172	52	100	30	23	32	237
173	28	100	62	20	27	237
174	43	85	57	23	29	237
175	41	88	38	38	32	237
176	58	90	30	30	30	238
177	20	100	55	31	32	238
178	43	100	55	11	29	238

Contd.

1	*2*	*3*	*4*	*5*	*6*	*7*
179	20	100	55	31	32	238
180	43	100	55	11	29	238
181	42	100	38	28	30	238
182	20	100	55	31	32	238
183	20	100	55	31	32	238
184	45	100	30	36	28	239
185	45	100	30	36	28	239
186	48	85	55	25	26	239
187	45	100	30	36	28	239
188	23	100	57	28	32	240
189	38	100	30	42	30	240
190	23	100	57	28	32	240
191	40	100	38	32	30	240
192	43	100	15	43	39	240
193	15	95	77	20	33	240
194	15	95	77	20	33	240
195	52	90	30	36	32	240
196	52	90	30	36	32	240
197	15	95	77	20	33	240
198	28	100	55	23	34	240
199	58	100	50	11	21	240
200	38	100	30	42	30	240
201	15	95	77	20	33	240
202	28	100	15	58	39	240
203	30	95	62	24	30	241
204	52	100	33	23	33	241
205	44	100	38	26	33	241
206	30	95	62	24	30	241
207	52	100	33	23	33	241
208	52	100	33	23	33	241
209	58	100	30	24	29	241
210	30	95	62	24	30	241

Contd.

1	*2*	*3*	*4*	*5*	*6*	*7*
211	52	100	0	56	33	241
212	46	95	33	33	35	242
213	43	100	43	30	26	242
214	40	85	57	35	25	242
215	43	100	43	30	26	242
216	43	100	43	30	26	242
217	46	95	33	33	35	242
218	46	95	33	33	35	242
219	40	85	57	35	25	242
220	20	100	62	28	33	243
221	20	100	62	28	33	243
222	54	100	30	30	30	244
223	45	100	33	34	32	244
224	43	88	43	40	30	244
225	43	88	43	40	30	244
226	43	88	43	40	30	244
227	45	100	33	34	32	244
228	48	85	57	25	30	245
229	50	88	30	44	33	245
230	48	85	57	25	30	245
231	60	90	38	23	34	245
232	48	85	57	25	30	245
233	48	85	57	25	30	245
234	48	85	57	25	30	245
235	48	85	57	25	30	245
236	48	88	60	21	30	247
237	33	100	62	21	31	247
238	39	100	55	23	30	247
239	41	83	55	41	28	248
240	46	88	38	47	29	248
241	40	100	50	25	33	248
242	54	83	55	25	32	249

Contd.

1	*2*	*3*	*4*	*5*	*6*	*7*
243	52	83	50	31	33	249
244	43	90	50	33	33	249
245	38	85	57	34	35	249
246	54	83	55	25	32	249
247	38	85	57	34	35	249
248	23	100	50	41	35	249
249	38	85	57	34	35	249
250	60	83	50	25	32	250
251	60	83	50	25	32	250
252	60	83	50	25	32	250
253	38	100	55	32	26	251
254	33	88	38	56	37	252
255	45	83	57	38	29	252
256	45	83	57	38	29	252
257	45	83	57	38	29	252
258	33	88	38	56	37	252
259	50	88	57	33	25	253
260	50	88	57	33	25	253
261	50	88	57	33	25	253
262	43	100	57	24	29	253
263	50	88	57	33	25	253
264	50	88	57	33	25	253
265	38	85	60	36	35	254
266	48	100	33	40	33	254
267	47	90	62	23	32	254
268	48	100	33	40	33	254
269	47	90	62	23	32	254
270	48	100	33	40	33	254
271	47	90	62	23	32	254
272	48	100	33	40	33	254
273	48	100	33	40	33	254
274	52	100	33	40	32	257

Contd.

1	*2*	*3*	*4*	*5*	*6*	*7*
275	52	100	33	40	32	257
276	38	100	50	38	32	258
277	44	90	50	23	51	258
278	49	95	50	33	31	258
279	32	100	50	41	35	258
280	52	85	50	38	33	258
281	38	100	50	38	32	258
282	30	100	55	24	49	258
283	38	100	55	32	34	259
284	41	100	55	33	30	259
285	46	88	57	38	30	259
286	55	100	57	20	27	259
287	55	100	57	20	27	259
288	46	88	57	38	30	259
289	46	88	57	38	30	259
290	73	100	33	18	36	260
291	60	100	60	14	26	260
292	40	100	30	53	37	260
293	73	100	33	18	36	260
294	60	100	60	14	26	260
295	73	100	33	18	36	260
296	55	100	33	41	33	262
297	55	100	33	41	33	262
298	55	100	33	41	33	262
299	49	100	62	19	32	262
300	55	100	33	41	33	262
301	61	100	38	31	32	262
302	49	100	62	19	32	262
303	55	100	33	41	33	262
304	61	100	38	31	32	262
305	41	100	55	31	36	263
306	41	100	55	31	36	263

Contd.

1	2	3	4	5	6	7
307	44	95	57	39	30	265
308	42	100	70	23	30	265
309	42	100	70	23	30	265
310	43	83	70	34	35	265
311	44	95	57	39	30	265
312	55	100	57	24	30	266
313	55	100	57	24	30	266
314	48	85	62	35	37	267
315	48	100	55	33	31	267
316	48	90	57	35	37	267
317	55	85	55	36	37	268
318	54	100	33	47	34	268
319	52	90	55	39	32	268
320	52	90	55	39	32	268
321	54	100	33	47	34	268
322	54	100	33	47	34	268
323	54	100	33	47	34	268
324	52	90	55	39	32	268
325	37	95	72	28	36	268
326	37	95	72	28	36	268
327	52	88	50	44	34	268
328	58	100	50	25	35	268
329	48	100	62	30	29	269
330	58	95	57	23	36	269
331	48	100	62	30	29	269
332	58	95	57	23	36	269
333	45	100	55	39	30	269
334	49	100	55	33	32	269
335	58	95	57	23	36	269
336	51	83	55	36	45	270
337	51	83	55	36	45	270
338	51	83	55	36	45	270

Contd.

1	*2*	*3*	*4*	*5*	*6*	*7*
339	51	83	55	36	45	270
340	51	83	55	36	45	270
341	64	100	33	44	30	271
342	64	100	33	44	30	271
343	64	100	33	44	30	271
344	61	100	52	24	35	272
345	48	88	60	38	38	272
346	48	88	60	38	38	272
347	61	100	52	24	35	272
348	58	100	55	25	36	274
349	61	100	57	31	26	275
350	58	85	55	48	29	275
351	61	100	57	24	33	275
352	43	100	60	36	36	275
353	65	90	30	56	34	275
354	61	100	57	31	26	275
355	58	85	55	48	29	275
356	61	100	57	31	26	275
357	61	100	57	31	26	275
358	61	100	57	31	26	275
359	61	100	57	24	33	275
360	61	100	57	24	33	275
361	48	100	60	40	29	277
362	48	100	60	40	29	277
363	52	100	55	35	35	277
364	45	100	50	52	32	279
365	45	85	70	48	31	279
366	48	83	86	28	36	281
367	48	83	86	28	36	281
368	68	100	75	38	0	281
369	58	85	55	49	35	282
370	54	100	62	36	30	282

Contd.

1	2	3	4	5	6	7
371	54	100	62	36	30	282
372	55	90	50	53	34	282
373	54	95	72	28	34	283
374	54	95	72	28	34	283
375	36	100	60	52	35	283
376	54	95	72	28	34	283
377	42	95	55	55	37	284
378	55	100	62	23	45	285
379	55	100	62	23	45	285
380	63	85	55	46	36	285
381	48	88	70	41	38	285
382	54	100	57	38	37	286
383	54	100	57	38	37	286
384	52	100	57	43	36	288
385	52	100	55	46	35	288
386	50	83	50	61	44	288
387	52	100	55	46	35	288
388	52	100	55	46	35	288
389	52	100	57	43	36	288
390	75	100	33	45	36	289
391	61	95	80	24	29	289
392	48	95	50	62	34	289
393	52	95	60	45	37	289
394	61	95	80	24	29	289
395	68	95	55	36	35	289
396	68	95	55	36	35	289
397	61	95	80	24	29	289
398	47	100	55	52	36	290
399	61	90	60	50	29	290
400	73	88	82	11	36	290
401	47	100	55	52	36	290
402	73	88	82	11	36	290

Contd.

1	*2*	*3*	*4*	*5*	*6*	*7*
403	47	100	55	52	36	290
404	55	100	50	44	42	291
405	55	100	50	44	42	291
406	55	100	50	44	42	291
407	58	100	55	50	30	293
408	51	95	62	46	39	293
409	51	95	62	46	39	293
410	58	100	55	50	30	293
411	58	100	55	50	30	293
412	60	95	38	62	40	295
413	52	100	55	56	33	296
414	47	100	55	58	37	297
415	64	83	60	52	38	297
416	47	100	55	58	37	297
417	47	100	55	58	37	297
418	64	100	62	38	34	298
419	64	100	62	38	34	298
420	64	100	62	38	34	298
421	70	100	70	25	34	299
422	73	95	57	43	31	299
423	54	100	75	38	33	300
424	54	100	75	38	33	300
425	63	100	55	44	39	301
426	58	100	75	36	33	302
427	58	100	57	53	34	302
428	58	100	57	53	34	302
429	58	100	57	53	34	302
430	55	95	82	31	39	302
431	58	100	57	53	34	302
432	58	100	57	53	34	302
433	55	95	82	31	39	302
434	55	95	82	31	39	302

Contd.

1	*2*	*3*	*4*	*5*	*6*	*7*
435	58	100	75	36	33	302
436	75	100	30	61	37	303
437	73	100	60	33	38	304
438	77	100	50	43	35	305
439	60	88	72	52	33	305
440	60	88	72	52	33	305
441	60	88	72	52	33	305
442	60	88	72	52	33	305
443	70	100	77	19	39	305
444	58	100	60	56	31	305
445	60	88	72	52	33	305
446	60	88	72	52	33	305
447	100	88	33	50	37	308
448	100	88	33	50	37	308
449	65	100	57	51	35	308
450	65	100	57	51	35	308
451	65	100	57	51	35	308
452	72	85	72	45	35	309
453	50	100	82	41	36	309
454	50	100	82	41	36	309
455	67	85	72	52	33	309
456	72	85	72	45	35	309
457	72	85	72	45	35	309
458	50	100	82	41	36	309
459	67	85	72	52	33	309
460	50	100	82	41	36	309
461	67	85	72	52	33	309
462	72	85	72	45	35	309
463	72	85	72	45	35	309
464	68	100	57	47	39	311
465	68	100	57	47	39	311
466	61	100	72	45	34	312

Contd.

1	*2*	*3*	*4*	*5*	*6*	*7*
467	61	100	72	45	34	312
468	75	100	38	56	44	313
469	75	100	38	56	44	313
470	75	100	38	56	44	313
471	72	100	77	33	32	314
472	72	100	77	33	32	314
473	68	100	75	38	38	319
474	68	100	77	41	35	321
475	65	100	55	60	41	321
476	68	100	77	41	35	321
477	72	88	77	49	37	323
478	72	88	77	49	37	323
479	72	88	77	49	37	323
480	60	100	60	61	42	323
481	83	100	57	40	43	323
482	72	88	77	49	37	323
483	83	100	57	40	43	323
484	100	100	30	59	39	328
485	61	100	77	53	38	329
486	61	100	77	53	38	329
487	77	95	72	39	47	330
488	77	95	72	39	47	330
489	77	95	72	39	47	330
490	77	95	72	39	47	330
491	64	100	70	60	38	332
492	77	100	55	61	40	333
493	100	90	70	40	38	338
494	90	90	70	60	31	341
495	73	100	72	58	41	344
496	73	100	72	58	41	344
497	73	100	72	58	41	344
498	73	100	72	58	41	344
499	90	85	70	80	38	363

APPENDIX-5

CONVERSION NORMS FOR MEN TEST

100 Mts. Run

Record Sec's	*Score Points*	*Record Sec's*	*Score Points*
17.4	10	14.6	51
17.3	13	14.5	52
17.2	15	14.4	53
17.1	18	14.3	54
17.0	20	14.2	54
16.9	23	14.1	55
16.8	25	14.0	58
16.7	28	13.9	60
16.6	30	13.8	61
16.5	32	13.7	63
16.4	33	13.6	64
16.3	35	13.5	65
16.2	36	13.4	67
16.1	37	13.3	68
16.0	38	13.2	70
15.9	39	13.1	72
15.8	40	13.0	73
15.7	41	12.9	75
15.6	42	12.8	77
15.5	43	12.7	78
15.4	44	12.6	80
15.3	45	12.5	83
15.2	46	12.4	85
15.1	47	12.3	88
15.0	48	12.2	90
14.9	49	12.1	95
14.8	50	12.0	100
14.7	51		

CONVERSION NORMS FOR MEN TEST

800 Mts. Run

Record Min., Sec.	*Score Points*	*Record Min., Sec.*	*Score Points*
2.59	10	2.28	54
2.58	13	2.27	55
2.57	15	2.26	56
2.56	18	2.25	57
2.55	20	2.24	58
2.53	23	2.23	59
2.52	25	2.22	60
2.51	28	2.21	61
2.50	30	2.20	62
2.49	32	2.19	64
2.48	33	2.18	65
2.47	35	2.17	66
2.46	36	2.16	67
2.45	37	2.15	68
2.44	38	2.14	69
2.43	39	2.13	70
2.42	40	2.12	72
2.41	41	2.11	73
2.40	42	2.10	75
2.39	43	2.09	77
2.38	44	2.08	78
2.37	45	2.07	80
2.36	46	2.07	80
2.35	47	2.06	83
2.34	48	2.05	85
2.33	49	2.04	88
2.32	50	2.03	89
2.31	51	2.02	90
2.30	52	2.01	95
2.29	53	2.00	100

CONVERSION NORMS FOR MEN TEST

High-Jump

Record Ft. Inc.	Score Points	Record Ft. Inc.	Score Points
3'6"	10	4'9"	62
3'61/2"	11	4'9.5"	64
3'7"	12	4'10"	65
3'7"	14	4'10.5"	66
3'8"	15	4'11"	67
3'8.5"	16	4'11.5"	69
3'9"	17	5'	70
3'9.5"	19	5'0.5"	71
3'10"	20	5'1"	72
3'10.5"	23	5'1.5"	74
3'11"	25	5'2"	75
3'11.5"	28	5'2.5"	76
4'	30	5'3"	77
4'1"	33	5'3.5"	79
4'1.5"	35	5'4"	80
4'2"	38	5'4.5"	81
4'2.5"	40	5'5"	82
4'3"	43	5'5.5"	83
4'3.5"	48	5'6"	84
4'4"	50	5'6.5"	85
4'4.5"	51	5'7"	86
4'5"	52	5'7.5"	87
4'5.5"	54	5'8"	89
4'6"	55	5'8.5"	90
4'6.5"	56	5'9"	93
4'7"	57	5'9.5"	95
4'7.5"	59	5'10"	98
4'8"	60	5'10.5"	100
4'8.5"	61		

CONVERSION NORMS FOR MEN TEST

Long-Jump

Record in Ft. Inc.	*Score Points*	*Record in Ft. Inc.*	*Score Points*	*Record in Ft. Inc.*	*Score Points*
10'	10	14'1"	41	17'6.5"	72
10'1"	11	14'2.5"	42	17'8"	73
10'1.5"	12	14'3.5"	43	17'10"	74
10'2"	13	14'5"	44	18"	75
10'3"	14	14'6"	45	18'2"	76
10'4"	15	14'7"	46	18'3.5"	77
10'6"	16	14'8"	47	18'5.5"	78
10'8"	17	14'9"	48	18'7"	79
10'11"	18	14'11"	49	18'10"	80
11'1"	19	15'	50	18'10.5"	81
11'3"	20	15'1.5"	51	19'	82
11'7"	21	15'3"	52	19'1"	83
11'11"	22	15'5"	53	19'2.5"	84
12'2"	23	15'6.5"	54	19'4"	85
12'6"	24	15'8"	55	19'6.5"	86
12'8"	25	15'9"	56	19'9"	87
12'10"	26	15'11"	57	19'11"	88
12'11"	27	16'	58	20'1.5"	89
13'	28	16'1.5"	59	20'4"	90
13'0.5"	29	16'3"	60	20'5.5"	91
13'1"	30	16'4"	61	20'7"	92
13'2"	31	16'5.5"	62	20'8"	93
13'3"	32	16'6.5"	63	20'9.5"	94
13'4"	33	16'8"	64	20'11"	95
13'5"	34	16'9"	65	21'1.5"	96
13'6"	35	16'10"	66	21'2"	97
13'7"	36	16'11"	67	21'3"	98
13'8.5"	37	17'1"	68	21'4.5"	99
13'9"	38	17'2"	69	21'6"	100
13'11"	39	17'3"	70		
14'	40	17'5"	71		

CONVERSION NORMS FOR MEN TEST

Shot Put (12 lbs)

Record in Mts. Ctm.	*Score Points*	*Record in Mts. Ctm.*	*Score Points*	*Record in Mts. Ctm.*	*Score Points*
1.50	10	7.20	41	13.70	72
1.60	11	7.40	42	14.00	73
1.70	12	7.60	43	14.30	74
1.80	13	7.80	44	14.60	75
1.90	14	8.00	45	14.90	76
2.00	15	8.20	46	15.20	77
2.20	16	8.40	47	15.50	78
2.40	17	8.60	48	15.90	79
2.60	18	8.80	49	16.20	80
2.80	19	9.00	50	16.50	81
3.00	20	9.20	51	16.80	82
3.20	21	9.40	52	17.10	83
3.40	22	9.60	53	17.40	84
3.60	23	9.80	54	17.60	85
3.80	24	10.00	55	17.80	86
4.00	25	10.20	56	18.00	87
4.20	26	10.40	57	18.20	88
4.40	27	10.60	58	18.40	89
4.60	28	10.80	59	18.60	90
4.80	29	11.00	60	18.80	91
5.00	30	11.20	61	18.90	92
5.20	31	11.40	62	19.00	93
5.40	32	11.60	63	19.10	94
5.60	33	11.80	64	19.20	95
5.80	34	12.00	65	19.30	96
6.00	35	12.20	66	19.40	97
6.20	36	12.40	67	19.50	98
6.40	37	12.60	68	19.60	99
6.60	38	12.80	69	19.70	100
6.80	39	13.10	70		
7.00	40	13.40	71		

APPENDIX-6

CONVERSION NORMS FOR WOMEN TEST

100 Mts. Run

Record Sec's	*Score Points*	*Record Sec's*	*Score Points*
19.4	10	16.6	51
19.3	13	16.5	52
19.2	15	16.4	53
19.1	18	16.3	54
18.1	20	16.2	54
18.9	23	16.1	55
18.8	25	16.0	58
18.7	28	15.9	60
18.6	30	15.8	61
18.5	32	15.7	63
18.4	33	15.6	64
18.3	35	15.5	65
18.2	36	15.4	67
18.1	37	15.3	68
18.0	38	15.2	70
17.9	39	15.1	72
17.8	40	15.0	73
17.7	41	14.9	75
17.6	42	14.8	77
17.5	43	14.7	78
17.4	44	14.6	80
17.3	45	14.5	83
17.2	46	14.4	85
17.1	47	14.3	88
17.0	48	14.2	90
16.9	49	14.1	95
16.8	50	14.0	100
16.7	51		

CONVERSION NORMS FOR WOMEN TEST

400 Mtrs. Run

Record Min's, Sec's	*Score Points*	*Record Min's, Sec's*	*Score Points*
1.56	10	1.29	51
1.55	13	1.28	52
1.54	15	1.27	53
1.53	18	1.26	54
1.52	20	1.25	55
1.51	23	1.24	58
1.50	25	1.23	60
1.49	28	1.22	61
1.48	30	1.21	63
1.47	32	1.20	64
1.46	33	1.19	65
1.45	35	1.18	67
1.44	36	1.17	68
1.43	37	1.16	70
1.42	38	1.15	72
1.41	39	1.14	73
1.40	40	1.13	75
1.39	41	1.12	77
1.38	42	1.11	78
1.37	43	1.10	80
1.36	44	1.09	83
1.35	45	1.00	85
1.34	46	1.07	88
1.33	47	1.06	90
1.31	49	1.04	100
1.30	50		

CONVERSION NORMS FOR WOMEN TEST

High-Jump

Record Ft. Inc.	*Score Points*	*Record Ft. Inc.*	*Score Points*
2'6"	10	3'9"	62
2'61/2"	11	3'9.5"	64
2'7"	12	3'10"	65
2'7"	14	3'10.5"	66
2'8"	15	3'11"	67
2'8.5"	16	3'11.5"	69
2'9"	17	4'	70
2'9.5"	19	4'0.5"	71
2'10"	20	4'1"	72
2'10.5"	23	4'1.5"	74
2'11"	25	4'2"	75
2'11.5"	28	4'2.5"	76
3'	30	4'3"	77
3'1"	33	4'3.5"	79
3'1.5"	35	4'4"	80
3'2"	38	4'4.5"	81
3'2.5"	40	4'5"	82
3'3"	43	4'5.5"	83
3'3.5"	48	4'6"	84
3'4"	50	4'6.5"	85
3'4.5"	51	4'7"	86
3'5"	52	4'7.5"	87
3'5.5"	54	4'8"	89
3'6"	55	4'8.5"	90
3'6.5"	56	4'9"	93
3'7"	57	4'9.5"	95
3'7.5"	59	4'10"	98
3'8"	60	4'10.5"	100
3'8.5"	61		

CONVERSION NORMS FOR WOMEN TEST

Long-Jump

Record in Ft. Inc.	*Score Points*	*Record in Ft. Inc.*	*Score Points*	*Record in Ft. Inc.*	*Score Points*
7'	10	11'1"	41	14'6.5"	72
7'1"	11	11'2.5"	42	14'8"	73
7'1.5"	12	11'3.5"	43	14'10"	74
7'2"	13	11'5"	44	15'	75
7'3"	14	11'6"	45	15'2"	76
7'4"	15	11'7"	46	15'3.5"	77
7'6"	16	11'8"	47	15'5.5"	78
7'8"	17	11'9"	48	15'7"	79
7'11"	18	11'11"	49	15'9"	80
8'1"	19	12'	50	15'10.5"	81
8'3"	20	12'1.5"	51	16'	82
8'7"	21	12'3"	52	16'1"	83
8'11"	22	12'5"	53	16'2.5"	84
9'2"	23	12'6.5"	54	16'4"	85
9'6"	24	12'8"	55	16'6.5"	86
9'8"	25	12'9"	56	16'9"	87
9'10"	26	12'11"	57	16'11"	88
9'12"	27	13'	58	17'1.5"	89
10'	28	13'1.5"	59	17'4"	90
10'0.5"	29	13'3"	60	17'5.5"	91
10'1"	30	13'4"	61	17'7"	92
10'2"	31	13'5.5"	62	17'8"	93
10'3"	32	13'6.5"	63	17'9.5"	94
10'4"	33	13'8"	64	17'11"	95
10'5"	34	13'9"	65	18'1.5"	96
10'6"	35	13'10"	66	18'2"	97
10'7"	36	13'11"	68	18'3"	98
10'8.5"	37	14'1"	68	18'4.5"	99
10'9"	38	14'2"	69	18'6"	100
10'11"	39	14'3"	70		
11'	40	14'5"	71		

CONVERSION NORMS FOR WOMEN TEST

Shot Put (8 lbs)

Record in Mts. Ctm.	*Score points*	*Record in Mts. Ctm.*	*Score points*	*Recrod in Mts. Ctm.*	*Score points*
1.50	10	7.20	41	13.70	72
1.60	11	7.40	42	14.00	73
1.70	12	7.60	43	14.30	74
1.80	13	7.80	44	14.60	75
1.90	14	8.00	45	14.90	76
2.00	15	8.20	46	15.20	77
2.20	16	8.40	47	15.50	78
2.40	17	8.60	48	15.90	79
2.60	18	8.80	49	16.20	80
2.80	19	9.00	50	16.50	81
3.00	20	9.20	51	16.80	82
3.20	21	9.40	52	17.10	83
3.40	22	9.60	53	17.40	84
3.60	23	9.80	54	17.60	85
3.80	24	10.00	55	17.80	86
4.00	25	10.20	56	18.00	87
4.20	26	10.40	57	18.20	88
4.40	27	10.60	58	18.40	89
4.60	28	10.80	59	18.60	90
4.80	29	11.00	60	18.80	91
5.00	30	11.20	61	18.90	92
5.20	31	11.40	62	19.00	93
5.40	32	11.60	63	19.10	94
5.60	33	11.80	64	19.20	95
5.80	34	12.00	65	19.30	96
6.00	35	12.20	66	19.40	97
6.20	36	12.40	67	19.50	98
6.40	37	12.60	68	19.60	99
6.60	38	12.80	69	19.70	100
6.80	39	13.10	70		
7.00	40	13.40	71